Intermediate Agility Workbook

by Clean Run Productions

An Eight-Week Training Program for Dogs That Have Completed an Introductory Agility Program

Clean Run Productions
35 Walnut Street, Turners Falls, MA 01376

Intermediate Agility Workbook

Second printing

Copyright © 1996, 1997 by Clean Run Productions

All Rights Reserved Worldwide. United States copyright law and international copyright treaties protect this book. Clean Run Productions depended on the availability of this protection when it decided to spend the time and money required to produce the handouts and teaching guidelines included in this publication. Nevertheless, Clean Run Productions realizes that you have purchased this book so that you can copy selected pages in their present or a modified form and share them with your students as well as other instructors who teach with you. The publisher therefore gives you permission to copy the forms, worksheets, handouts, instructor notes, and student notes included in this publication for your own *internal* use. However, you may not make copies of any portion of this book for commercial distribution or resale and you may not include information from this book in a secondary product that is to be commercially distributed.

Published by **Clean Run Productions**
35 Walnut Street
Turners Falls, MA 01376-2317
413/863-8303

Acquiring Editor and Chief Writer   Bud Houston
Editors and Contributors   Linda Mecklenburg and Monica Percival
Book and Cover Design   Monica Percival
Cover Artwork   Jo Ann Mather, and Valerie Pietraszewska
Book Illustrations   Jaci Cotton, Karen Gaydos, Nancy Krouse-Culley, Bud Houston, Jo Ann Mather, Pascal Peng, and Valerie Pietraszewska
Printing   Hadley Printing Company

ISBN 0-9653994-1-9

Limits of Liability and Disclaimer of Warranty
The author, editors, and publisher shall not be liable in the event of incidental or consequential damages in connection with, or arising out of, the furnishing, performance, or use of the instructions and suggestions contained in this book.

Copyright
All service marks, trademarks, and product names used in this publication belong to their respective holders; including or in addition to the following:

USDAA® and Agility Dog® are registered service marks of the United States Dog Agility Association, Inc.

AKC® is a registered trademark of the American Kennel Club, Inc.

Contents

Program Director's Notes

This workbook represents an eight-week instruction for dogs that have previously been introduced to the sport of dog agility and the obstacles used in this sport, either through the program described in the *Introductory Agility Workbook* by Clean Run Productions or a comparable introductory course. The exercises and discussions here are intended for the instructors of an intermediate program. Pages are included that are suitable for handout material for the students in the program.

Objectives of This Intermediate Program

The objective of this program is to instill confidence and a sense of fun in performing agility obstacles in short sequences for your intermediate dogs and handlers. This program places a fundamental emphasis on the handler keeping the dog's attention at all times. While sequencing is important in an intermediate program, the design of this instruction asks for the dog's attention first, pushing forward only when the dog is giving that attention. This program also emphasizes the following training concepts:

- The handler will reward his dog for the performance of a contact obstacle in the descending contact zone and nowhere else. The dog is not allowed to leave the contact zone of the obstacle without the permission, a quiet release command, of the handler.

- The handler will be challenged to perform what are generally considered advanced handling maneuvers. In reality, these maneuvers are more easily learned early in a handler's training and will prove more important in the long run than focusing only on running longer and longer sequences.

- The dog will be encouraged to go away from the handler to work.

- Your students will be frequently presented with exercises that are calculated to break the habit of working the dog in heel position.

NOTE: Basic training methodologies for obstacle performance are *not* discussed in this workbook as they are covered in detail in the *Introductory Agility Workbook* published by Clean Run Productions.

About the Logistics of an Intermediate Program

While the presentation in this workbook may appear to suggest or endorse the one right way to conduct an intermediate program, training programs for dog agility take a variety of forms. Programs differ in terms of basic training techniques, administration, length of program, and guidelines for admittance and graduation.

Guidelines for Admittance
Dogs are eligible for this intermediate program when:

- **The dog has successfully completed an approved introductory agility program.** If a dog and handler did not complete *your* introductory agility program, make sure you find out details about their prior agility training and assess whether or not they have an appropriate background for making the transition to your intermediate program. If you have any reservations about a student, you may want to consider requiring the student to take a private lesson with you. This will allow you to better acquaint yourself with both handler and dog, and give the handler a chance to familiarize himself with your training techniques.

- **You have received a complete application and pre-payment of the training fee.** Prior to the first class, the dog's owner should have submitted an application for enrollment, which should include the owner's signature, a release of liability, and proof of current vaccinations. Be sure you have a clearly stated policy regarding refunds (if any) for cancellation.

- **The dog demonstrates basic control.** As in the introductory agility program, this should be determined as a pre-assessment. There may be graduates from your introductory class who do not have enough control when their dogs are off-lead to handle an intermediate agility class without disrupting your entire program. It's probably best to refer these students to a basic obedience class since they need to focus on control.

Guidelines for Graduation

This program is designed so that it *can* be repeated. To graduate from this program to an advanced agility program, the dog should be able to demonstrate basic proficiency on all of the obstacles and should be able to work off-lead without the handler losing control.

You have to remember that some handlers will take a requirement to repeat the intermediate class as being "held back" or "flunked". You are obligated to present this requirement to your students in a more positive manner. Some dogs do not progress as quickly as other dogs. A dog's chances for long term success rest upon attention to solid fundamental training. It is better to go slowly early in a dog's training. Advancing the dog into a program where he *will* ultimately fail, will be detrimental to the dog's agility career.

You could require a title from any agility organization or a qualifying leg to graduate into the advanced class. By setting such a requirement, the criteria for advancement would be clear-cut and fairly applied. However, the difficulty in setting this kind of requirement to advance is that a) your intermediate classes would get very large as they fill up with students waiting for that first qualifying leg; and b) you would need to have a structured process to raise the jump height of dogs to competition height. That process is *not* reflected in this workbook.

What Your Students Should Bring to Class

When you confirm a dog's enrollment in your training program, use the opportunity to remind your students what they need to bring to class. Here's a good list for you to work with:

*   A buckle collar or a quick release collar.

*   A 4" or 6" tab lead.

*   A 6' obedience lead.

*   Lots of the dog's favorite food treats. Some people don't really know what their dog's favorite treat is. If you assess that a dog isn't particularly interested in the food motivator selected by his handler, suggest that the handler bring a *special* treat such as string cheese, Rollover™, Oinkeroll™, microwaved hotdogs, liver, etc.

*   A toy motivator (such as a ball, a Frisbee™, or a squeaky toy).

*   Water and a bowl for the dog.

*   A hungry dog! For an evening agility class, recommend that your students delay the dog's dinner until after class. For classes earlier in the day, they should skip the dog's morning feeding. This tactic will make the dog's attention that much keener!

NOTE: Along with their confirmation notice, send each student a copy of the handout on page 12 about training weave poles at home.

How to Divide Your Classes

Each class session in this workbook has three working "sets". A set is the collection of equipment for which one instructor is responsible during the class. It is usually better, though certainly not required, for one instructor to remain with the same set of equipment throughout the class. The students, divided into groups, rotate from set to set during the class. Divide your class evenly—one group of students for each set.

The sets are intended to be worked simultaneously by a large class or consecutively by a small class. If you are working sets simultaneously, it's necessary to divide your students into logical groups. The best way to divide a class is by jump height. This allows dogs of the same jump height to work together so not a lot of time is spent adjusting bars.

NOTE: Throughout this workbook we make reference to "big dogs" and "little dogs". In general, any dog that measures 16" or less at the shoulders is considered a little dog. Any dog measuring more than 16" is a big dog.

Another way to divide a class is by skill level. For example, if you use the data on the Progress Worksheets in this book to group together the dogs having difficulty with certain skills, it will be possible to fashion a more remedial program for just those dogs. Dogs that are advancing more quickly can be given a more advanced program.

If you divide into groups, the time students spend on each set should be carefully monitored; otherwise, it's possible that there won't be enough time to get to all the required sets. To make this work, one of your instructors must be assigned the task of keeping time. If there are three sets and three groups of students, for example, an hour should be divided into 20-minute working periods. The timekeeper will give a two-minute warning *prior* to each switch between sets and will announce clearly at the end of the 20 minutes that it is time to switch.

Setting Up for Class

From day one, be an advocate for teaching your students the proper work ethic for participation in this sport. Setting up equipment is a lot of work. Get your students involved. If you get them used to the idea that you're going to do everything for them, they will soon come to expect you to continue to do so. Get them used to doing a share of the work and they will always expect to do their fair share.

One possibility is to require half of the class to come 30 minutes early to help move and set up equipment. Require the other half of the class to stay late to put equipment away and clean up the training site. Be prepared to get tough with students who won't do their fair share of work. Make them sit out a week if they don't help with the work!

Cleaning Up After the Dogs

Encourage your students to exercise their dogs before coming to class. However, accidents are sometimes unavoidable. Your policy should be that the handler is responsible for immediately cleaning up after his dog.

Some programs require that students always be prepared for such an accident by carrying at least one plastic baggie in a pocket at all times. This ensures that the mess is quickly cleaned up and that it's not "lost" or stepped in while the handler is searching the training site for cleaning implements.

Not Allowed!

By policy, you should not allow:

- **Aggressive dogs.** Dogs should not exhibit aggressiveness either towards other dogs or towards people.

- **Harsh training methods.**

- **Choke chains and pinch collars.**

- **Bitches in season.** Some clubs do not allow bitches in heat. Other clubs can function adequately if the bitch is diapered. You'll have to make the call.

- **Barking dogs.** Of course, all dogs bark. What you are guarding against here is the dog that barks without pause or purpose. This restriction is intended to placate neighbors that would be disturbed by a constantly barking animal as well as to make sure that instructors aren't struggling to be heard over the noise.

- **Dogs that run away.** If you can't catch 'em, you can't train 'em.

Don't Forget Your Instructors

Being an instructor is sometimes a thankless job. Often instructors train other people's dogs at the expense of training their own. We advocate a policy that sets aside time and facilities for instructors to put their own dogs on the equipment. In an ideal world, your instructors should receive financial compensation for sharing their expertise and expending time and effort in support of your training program. An unpaid instructor can soon become an unhappy instructor.

How to Use This Workbook

This workbook includes pages that are designed for you to copy and distribute to your instructors and your students. For each week of the program, you will find student and instructor handouts, Progress Worksheets, and Facility Layouts that you can copy. The following sections explain how to best use each of these tools.

Handouts

This workbook is designed so that pages can be copied as handouts. Handouts come in two forms:

- **Student Handouts**—Each week have ready for your students the pages labeled "Student Notes". Remember that your students will be avidly interested in anything they can get their hands on to read about this sport.

- **Instructor Handouts**—For each week of class, each instructor should receive the "Instructor Notes" with the Progress Worksheet for that week copied on the second side. Each instructor should also receive a copy of the exercise(s) for which he'll be responsible. Ideally, the instructors should receive their copies *at least* a week ahead of the scheduled class so they can mentally prepare for what they must do with their students.

  Instructors should get a copy of the Facility Layout for that week so they can direct the work in setting up the equipment for that lesson.

  Encourage your instructors to make notes about what works *and* what doesn't work in the training program. Your program will improve by the empirical knowledge they earn while conducting classes. An instructor will develop a keener eye for training and performance issues by keeping copious notes on the process.

Progress Worksheets

On the back of each week's Instructor Notes is a worksheet—or if you prefer, a model for a worksheet—that is used to take attendance and track a dog's progress with the exercises. The worksheets help you remember who needs help and in what areas. Remind your instructors that they should be making notes that will help you determine who should be doing the more advanced exercises and who should be moving along more slowly.

Each week write the names of your students in the left column, along with their dogs' names. This will help you and the other instructors learn all the new names you need to learn. It will also help you track attendance over the course of the program and assist your instructors in setting the difficulty of the exercises each week.

Facility Layouts and Facility Layout Worksheets

The Facility Layout is a design for placement of the obstacles on your training field. Some thought has been given to the ideal placement of the obstacles in the field, considering how dogs will move through each exercise and how dogs and their handlers might line up or queue at the start of each set.

In an ideal world, we all have two acres in which to set up our training sets. In the real world, however, many clubs do their training in limited spaces. It's conceivable that there won't be enough space to set up all exercises for a given week at the same time. If your agility area is smaller than the ideal field, you must design the facility layout for each week *prior* to class. For this reason, blank Facility Layout Worksheets have been provided. Feel free to make additional copies for your use.

Designing the facility layout is no small task, you will find. You have to be very thoughtful about how the obstacles are going to be set up. There should be enough room between sets so that dogs are not running into each other. This will be especially important when dogs are working off-lead. Consider too that only one dog will be working on a set at a time. You must leave room for dogs and their handlers to wait in line, and you must leave room for some kind of path for a dog finishing an exercise to get back to the end of the line.

Acknowledgments

We thank all of the people who have made contributions to this *Intermediate Agility Workbook*. A special thanks to Linda Mecklenburg and Monica Percival whose considerable skill and insight as agility instructors and seminar leaders are reflected in the philosophy of this book. We also want to say thanks to a wonderful corps of artists who have allowed us to use their work to brighten up these pages: Jaci Cotton, Karen Gaydos, Jo Ann Mather, Nancy Krouse-Culley, Pascal Peng, and Valerie Pietraszewska.

Curriculum

Most of your students will be fresh out of the introductory training program. In *that* program, the dogs were introduced to the obstacles and little more. In the intermediate training program, you will introduce the dog and handler to sequencing and some important handling concepts, ranging from elementary to advanced.

Some dogs and their handlers will progress at a more aggressive pace than others. You may also have some students in class who are repeating the intermediate program. Consequently, your program has to be adaptable to dogs progressing at different speeds. Your instructors should be able to simplify exercises for dogs that are struggling and add complexity to exercises for dogs that are progressing quickly and are ready for new challenges.

This curriculum incorporates the performance and handling concepts listed below. More advanced concepts are denoted with a paw print: 🐾 This symbol is used throughout this workbook to denote advanced exercises.

- Basic obedience

- Consistent performance of contact obstacles, weave poles, and the table

- Working on both sides of the dog

- Leading out from the dog to start an exercise

- Sending the dog away to perform an obstacle

- Using *Come!* to change direction

- Introduction of the spread hurdle

- Changing sides to the dog while the dog is on the table

- Using *Get Out!* to change direction 🐾

- Performing a 180° turn 🐾

- Changing sides to the dog while the dog is in a tunnel 🐾

- Changing sides to the dog while the dog is jumping 🐾

This might seem like a lot to accomplish. But given that it's delivered over a period of eight weeks, it is actually a fairly modest list.

Artist: Jaci Cotton

The following table summarizes the three sets you will work during each week of the eight-week program as well as the equipment that is required for each set.

	Set 1	Set 2	Set 3
Week 1	**Speed Up—Long Jump Review** **Send to Table** 🐾 *Obstacles Required:* three winged jumps, long jump, pipe tunnel, table *Note:* Minor equipment movement is required between exercises.	**Spread Hurdle and A-Frame** **Tire and See-Saw** **Collapsed Tunnel and Dogwalk** **Weave Poles** *Obstacles Required:* spread hurdle, A-frame, tire, see-saw, collapsed tunnel, dogwalk, weave poles	**Simple Sequencing** **Speed Circle** *Obstacles Required:* five winged jumps *Note:* Major equipment movement is required between exercises.
Week 2	**A.D.D. Tunnel Exercise** **Blind to Spread Hurdle** *Obstacles Required:* pipe tunnel, tire, spread hurdle, collapsed tunnel	**Inside-Out Contacts** **Dogwalk Straightover** *Obstacles Required:* A-frame, winged jump, see-saw, weave poles, dogwalk, table	**Send to Jump** **Speed Circle** **Branching Path** 🐾 *Obstacles Required:* five winged jumps, long jump *Note:* Major equipment movement is required between exercises.
Week 3	**Double and Tunnel** **Looping Sequence** 🐾 *Obstacles Required:* pipe tunnel, tire, collapsed tunnel, see-saw, two winged jumps	**Can Your Dog Really Weave?** 🐾 **Over and Back** *Obstacles Required:* weave poles, table, spread jump, long jump, one winged jump, dogwalk, pipe tunnel	**Send to Jump** **Speed Circle** **Options** 🐾 *Obstacles Required:* five winged jumps, A-frame *Note:* Major equipment movement is required between exercises.
Week 4	**Weave Poles and Tunnel** **Reversing Flow** *Obstacles Required:* pipe tunnel, weave poles, A-frame, dogwalk, see-saw, long jump, one winged jump	**Half Circle Sequence** **Blind Cross** 🐾 *Obstacles Required:* pipe tunnel, spread hurdle, one winged jump, tire, collapsed tunnel *Note:* Minor equipment movement is required between exercises.	**Send to Jump** **Speed Circle Variation** **Static Cross** 🐾 *Obstacles Required:* five winged jumps, table *Note:* Major equipment movement is required between exercises.
Week 5	**Anticipation** *Obstacles Required:* two winged jumps, weave poles, table, pipe tunnel	**Collapsed Turn** *Obstacles Required:* collapsed tunnel, long jump, one winged jump	**Working Flows** *Obstacles Required:* A-frame, spread hurdle, dogwalk, see-saw, tire, four winged jumps
Week 6	**Little Feets** **Tunnel Side-Track** 🐾 *Obstacles Required:* tire, spread hurdle, two winged jumps, pipe tunnel *Note:* Minor equipment movement is required between exercises.	**Fast Flow to Weaves** **Dogwalk Sequence** *Obstacles Required:* weave poles, two winged jumps, long jump, dogwalk *Note:* Minor equipment movement is required between exercises.	**Send to Table** **Off-Side Conditioning** **Horseshoe** *Obstacles Required:* table, collapsed tunnel, A-frame, five winged jumps *Note:* Minor equipment movement is required between exercises.
Week 7	**Turning Game** **A Change of Sides** *Obstacles Required:* Four winged jumps, spread hurdle, collapsed tunnel, tire	**Working the Outside** **To Boldly Go** *Obstacles Required:* Dogwalk, table, A-frame, two winged jumps, weave poles	**The Wave** **Turn Backs** *Obstacles Required:* See-saw, pipe tunnel, three winged jumps *Note:* Minor equipment movement is required between exercises.
Week 8	**Dynamic Cross** **Blind to Long Jump** 🐾 *Obstacles Required:* Dogwalk, long jump, see-saw, weave poles, three winged jumps, collapsed tunnel *Note:* Minor equipment movement is required between exercises.	**Perch in the Speed Circle** **Sheep Shank** 🐾 *Obstacles Required:* three winged jumps, spread hurdle, table *Note:* Minor equipment movement is required between exercises.	**Ready Freddy!** **Freddy Inside Out** 🐾 *Obstacles Required:* A-frame, pipe tunnel, tire, two winged jumps *Note:* Minor equipment movement is required between exercises.

Intermediate Agility Workbook

Raising Obstacles During the Curriculum

In the *Introductory Agility Workbook*, we gave you very specific guidelines for setting the height of the obstacles each week. In this program, we are instead going to give you goals to work towards during the eight weeks. Ultimately, *you* need to decide when to increase the difficulty of an obstacle. You'll make this decision based on the dogs' progress with each obstacle and also the "adjustability" of your obstacles. For example, if you have jumps that adjust in 1" or 2" increments, you could raise the jumps 2" each week. If, however, your jumps adjust in only 4" or 6" increments, you need to wait until you think the dogs are ready to make a step that large.

Another factor that may influence your decision will be the amount of time that elapses between a dog completing the introductory program and beginning the intermediate. For example, if you teach in the Northeast and don't have an indoor training facility for the winter, it's conceivable that your introductory graduates may have to wait five months to start an intermediate program. In this case, you cannot expect the dogs to be comfortable with where they left off with the obstacles in the introductory program. For the first couple of weeks of the intermediate program, you may need to set the obstacles lower than the minimum heights we recommend here.

Dogwalk

If you used an adjustable dogwalk in the introductory program, we recommended that you didn't raise it above 3'. For the first few weeks of the intermediate program, keep the dogwalk at 3'. If dogs are doing well, raise it to 42" in Week 4. Then raise the walk to 48" in Week 5 and keep it at that height for the duration of the program.

A-Frame

In Week 8 of the introductory program, your students worked with the A-frame at 4-1/2'. For Week 1 of the intermediate program, keep the A-frame at 4-1/2'. If the dogs are doing well, raise the A-frame to 5' in Week 2. Then raise the apex to 5-1/2' in Week 4 and to 6' for the duration of the program.

See-Saw

In the introductory program, your students trained with a regulation see-saw. However, it may be necessary to review several steps of the training program to ensure that dogs are comfortable initiating the tip of the plank.

Jumps and Tire Jump

At the end of the introductory program, big dogs were jumping 12" and little dogs were jumping 6". By the end of the intermediate program, dogs should ideally be jumping 6" below their *regulation* jump height. For Week 1 of the program, keep the jumps at 6" for little dogs and 12" for big dogs. If your jumps adjust in 1"or 2" increments and all the dogs are comfortable, start raising the jumps in Week 2. If your jumps adjust only in 4" or 6" increments, wait until Week 4 to increase the jump heights and then consider another increase in Week 6 or 7.

Long Jump

At the end of the introductory program, big dogs were jumping three planks with a 30" spread and little dogs two planks with a 20" spread. A bar jump was placed between *each* of the planks. For Weeks 1 and 2 of the intermediate program, keep the long jump set this way. In Week 2, however, remove the bar jumps. In Week 3, use four planks with a 40" spread for big dogs and three planks with a 30" spread for little dogs (except for 12" jumpers who should jump only two planks with a 20" spread). If any big dogs are having problems with four planks, put a bar jump between the two middle planks. You can remove the bar jump later.

Table

At the end of the introductory program, the table was set at 12" for little dogs and 18" for big dogs. In Week 1 of the intermediate program, keep the table set at these heights. In Week 2, raise the table 6" (except for 12" jumpers) so that all but 30" jumpers are using a table at their regulation height.

Weave Poles

For this program, we recommend using channel wires. A detailed explanation is provided on page 17.

Tunnels

By the end of the introductory program, the dogs had worked with the pipe tunnel in many different configurations and with a 12' long chute on the collapsed tunnel. Most dogs should still be comfortable with the pipe tunnel whether it's straight or bent. If not, do a short review with this obstacle. For the collapsed tunnel, however, start with an 8' long chute in Week 1. If the dogs are comfortable, introduce the 12' chute in Week 2.

Training Weave Poles at Home

Weave pole performance has made or broken many an agility run. Besides being the most difficult obstacle for the dog to learn, we require a very complicated and specific performance from our dogs. Not only do we want our dogs to make the correct entry to the poles, we also want them to alternately weave down the line of poles regardless of how many poles we put up. And, by the way, we want them to do it fast.

Unlike USDAA® and NADAC novice tests, AKC® novice tests do not include weave poles. However, even if you plan on competing exclusively in AKC, it is a mistake to ignore training for this obstacle until you reach the Open class. If your dog is promoted into Open not really knowing how to weave, you are in for a long, tough campaign. It is much simpler to teach your dog the weave poles from day one.

Your dog will *not* learn to weave working only one hour a week in an eight-week class. Teaching your dog to weave requires more repetitions than you can possibly do in class where you're trying to master *all* of the obstacles, not just the poles. Your dog will learn to weave by weaving. You need to have poles set up at home.

In your first intermediate agility class, your instructor is going to tell you about a game called Weave Pole Knockout. You'll get a chance to play this game during the fifth week of class. However, you really need to practice your weave poles **every day** so that you can be prepared for this competition. Otherwise, you could be embarrassed by your dog's performance. (You don't want *that* to happen).

There are many types of weave poles and weave pole training devices available commercially. While some of these devices are expensive, they are easy and convenient to set up and use. If you're interested, your instructor should be able to give you information on companies that make equipment. If, however, you aren't yet ready to make that financial plunge, there are several types of poles you can make at home yourself.

Leaning Poles

The easiest kind of poles to make are ones that you stick in the ground. Cut steel rebar into 2' long pieces and drive them into the ground at regular intervals (between 20" to 22"). Now, slide a 3' long piece of 3/4" i.d. PVC pipe over each section of rebar. When you stick the poles in the ground, the first pole leans left, the second pole leans right, and so on down to the end of the line so that your dog can see a channel through the poles.

If you don't have facilities to cut rebar or PVC, you can set up leaning poles in your yard using tomato stakes, electric fence posts (visit your local farm store), driveway markers, or any type of post you can find that is approximately 3/4" to 1" in diameter and 3' long.

Weave Pole Chute

If you don't have enough yard space to do weave pole training, you could do it in the house. For example, you could purchase six bathroom plungers and make a weave pole chute down the hallway. Instead of leaning the poles, you just stagger them left and right. Over time you bring the poles together to form a straight line.

Channel Wires

Make some poles to stick in the ground as previously described. Instead of putting the poles in the ground at an angle, put them in standing straight up. Then connect the poles as shown in the diagram using 5' lengths of 12 or 14 gauge wire. Coil the ends of the wire around the poles. The wire should be at the dog's shoulder height. If the wire won't stay in place by itself, use plastic garbage bag ties or electrical ties to hold the wires in place on the poles. Notice that the odd poles are connected and the even poles are connected so that the dog has a perfect channel, defined by the wires, down the length of the weave poles.

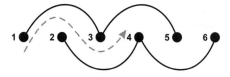

Some dogs will try to jump over the wires or run under them. To prevent this, you can use two sets of wires—one high and one low—so that they guard against the dog passing through.

Week 1: Instructor Notes

One thing you can be certain of as you begin your intermediate training program is that dogs will not be proficient with certain obstacles. This is especially true of the see-saw, the tire, and the weave poles. While the dogs were introduced to these obstacles in the introductory program, few dogs will be competent yet in performing them. Indeed, at this point in training, there is no obstacle that *some dog* in your class might not have problems with.

You have to keep in mind that *confidence* is what agility training is all about. You have to resist pushing ahead to more complicated exercises while basic obstacle performance issues are still a problem. Refer to the Appendix for a discussion of remedial fixes for problems with individual obstacles.

Go as slowly as you need to for individual students. Keep your training upbeat. Make it fun for the dogs *and* for the humans. Always end an exercise on a positive note, even if you have to simplify the exercise.

Artist: Jo Ann Mather

	Set 1	Set 2	Set 3
Week 1	**Speed Up—Long Jump Review** **Send to Table** 🐾 *Obstacles Required:* three winged jumps, long jump, pipe tunnel, table *Note:* Minor equipment movement is required between exercises.	**Spread Hurdle and A-Frame** **Tire and See-Saw** **Collapsed Tunnel and Dogwalk** **Weave Poles** *Obstacles Required:* spread hurdle, A-frame, tire, see-saw, collapsed tunnel, dogwalk, weave poles	**Simple Sequencing** **Speed Circle** *Obstacles Required:* five winged jumps *Note:* Major equipment movement is required between exercises.

Organizational Notes

Start the new class with introductions all around. As your students introduce themselves, check them "present" on the Progress Worksheet (on the other side of this page). Don't forget to introduce yourself.

After you've welcomed your students and taken care of various housekeeping items, tell them about the Week 5 Weave Pole Knockout competition. Remind them that they will need to be working on the weave poles at home to prepare for this competition.

Remind all the instructors to mark the Progress Worksheet if any students are having trouble.

Start the training session by doing the control exercise on page 17 with *all* students. Then break into groups for the training sets, if you're going to work multiple sets simultaneously.

NOTE: Set 3 will require major equipment movement between exercises.

Week 1: Progress Worksheet

Instructors: **Date:**

Handler and Dog	Present	Notes

GENERAL NOTES:

Week 1: Facility Layout

One square = 10'

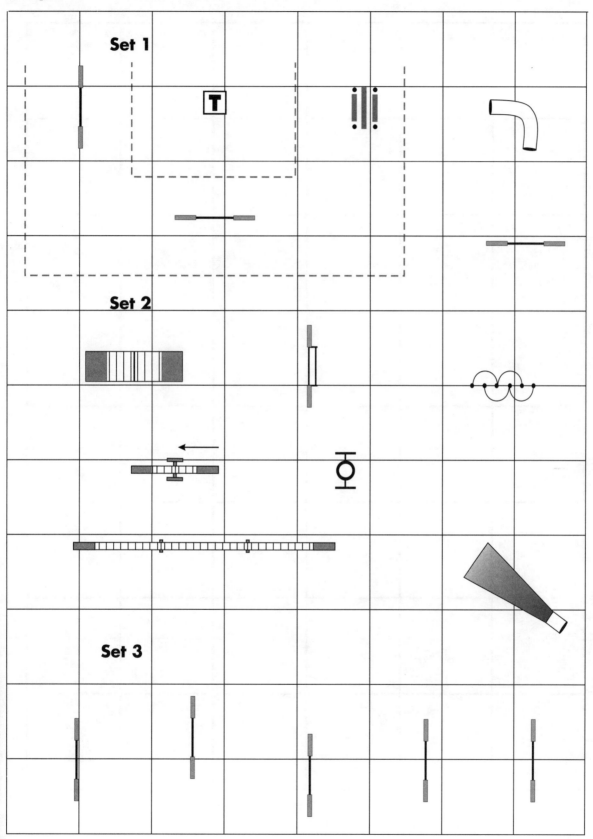

Set 1

Set 2

Set 3

WEEK 1

Week 1: Facility Layout Worksheet

Design your Facility Layout using a 1" = 10' scale (standard agility template)

16   Intermediate Agility Workbook

Week 1: Exercises

Start the class by doing the control exercise with everyone. Then break into smaller groups if you're going to work the training sets simultaneously.

Control Exercise

Start the session with an obedience exercise to call everyone's attention to the basic control commands. Many students will have done basic obedience with their dogs, but others may have no concept of simple skills like *Sit!* and *Stay!* and *Come!* If there is a control problem with particular dogs, this exercise will make it clear.

NOTE: Any dogs who cannot behave off-lead during this exercise should be put back on-leash immediately.

* Working the dogs *off-lead* and in heel position, heel everybody through the obstacle course. Instruct the lead handler to weave a random course among the obstacles.

* Halt and *Sit!* the dogs. Have handlers leave their dogs and walk out about 10'. Turn back to face the dogs. Hold that position for about 30 seconds and instruct everyone to return to their dogs.

* Heel about again, stretching your students into a long line along one edge of the agility field. Halt and *Down!* the dogs. Have handlers leave their dogs and walk out about 10'. Turn back to face the dogs.

* After a minute, recall the dogs—*Fluffy Come!*

At the end of this exercise, you might want to make a short speech about doing homework. The basic control commands (*Come! Sit! Down!* and *Stay!*) should be reviewed at home frequently and consistently.

Make a note on your Progress Worksheet for dogs having difficulty with control.

About the Weave Poles

Okay, here's a problem for you. You've just started a new intermediate class with fifteen students fresh out of the introductory program. Your mission: Teach their dogs to weave. You have eight weeks to get it done during one class hour a week.

The dogs were "introduced" to the weave poles in their introductory agility class. But the poles were leaning at such an angle, or channeled open so wide, that they hardly resembled weave poles. Needless to say, these dogs will *not* know how to weave when they begin your class. So, how are you going to do it? How will you teach all these dogs to weave when you only have them for an hour, once a week?

Answer: You're not. (As in, forget it...no way...can't be done...)

Instead, you're going to make an important homework assignment in the first class—you'll charge your students to teach their dogs to weave at home. To give them incentive to work on this assignment, we'll borrow a training technique from Janet Gauntt, an instructor for the Artful Dodgers in Baltimore, Maryland. Let your students know that in the fifth week of class, there will be a Weave Pole Knockout competition. We'll do this for the express purpose of embarrassing your students into taking their at-home weave pole training seriously.

During the introductory program, we recommended using leaning poles in class. This was to encourage enthusiasm and get dogs comfortable with the weaving action itself. For this intermediate program, the focus will be on teaching entry and accuracy. So in class, we recommend using only regulation weave poles with channel wires; there will be no staggered poles or leaning poles at the training site. Having the wires on the poles means the handler isn't required to set up the dog every time and forces *the dog* to be responsible for correct entry. By sheer repetition, the dog will learn to confidently enter the poles and always enter with the first pole on his left.

At home, handlers may use either slanted poles or channel wires to continue their training. However, they may find it easier to set up a permanent set of poles with wires than to hammer poles into the ground at an angle. If there are students who weren't in your introductory program, you may want to give them copies of the Student Notes from the *Introductory Agility Workbook* that discuss teaching weave poles at home.

WEEK 1

Set 1

Your set consists of two exercises that use the same equipment. Between exercises, however, you will need to replace the long jump with a bar jump. The "Send to Table" exercise is a bit advanced. If it's more than most of your students are ready to deal with, simplify the exercise so that it results in a positive and successful experience.

Speed Up—Long Jump Review

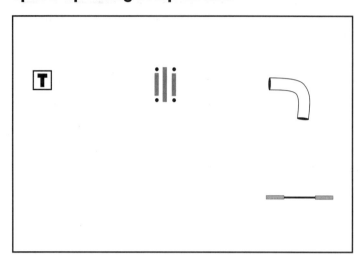

This simple sequence sets up a nice flow when run in either direction.

1. Starting with the dog on the table, each handler performs this sequence: long jump–tunnel–bar jump.

2. After the jump, the handler praises and treats the dog, and then immediately turns around and performs the sequence in reverse. Because of the left turn in the sequence when it's reversed, the dog should now be working on the handler's right. The handler praises and treats the dog when it finishes on the table.

NOTE: Working with the dog on the right (the "off-side") can be disconcerting for novice handlers who have obedience trained their dogs. Use this opportunity to talk about the benefits of being able to handle a dog on the right. When this sequence is reversed, the dog should be compelled to take the longer path and the handler should take the shorter, inside path. It's significant that the handler will be able to move faster in relationship to the dog. This means that the dog has to run faster to keep up.

3. Repeat steps 1 and 2 several times.

4. Starting at the bar jump with the dog on his right, each handler performs this sequence: bar jump–tunnel–long jump–table.

5. The handler praises and treats his dog on the table, and then immediately turns around and performs the sequence in reverse order. The dog should now be on the handler's left. Make sure the handler praises and treats the dog when it finishes the sequence over the jump.

6. Repeat steps 4 and 5 several times.

During each repetition, work with your students on all of the following:

*   Keeping an erect posture—even for a small dog, a handler does not need to crouch down and hover in order for the dog to be able to see him—and facing in the direction of the flow.

*   Giving a hand signal and command for each obstacle. Remind students to use the arm closest to the obstacle and to time their commands so that the dog has plenty of notice of each obstacle.

*   Getting the dog moving as fast as possible to clear the long jump. This is in the handler's best interest *anytime* a hurdle with a dimension of depth is in front of the dog. In this exercise, if your students can send their dogs ahead to the tunnel after the jump, the handler can take a short cut towards the long jump. When the dog emerges from the tunnel, the handler will be out in front and the dog will have to hurry to catch up.

*   Working on a *Down!* or *Sit!* on the table. On the first two repetitions, students should reward the dog just for getting on the table. On *subsequent* repetitions, alternate asking the dogs to *Down!* or *Sit!* on the table. Your students should reward the dog immediately upon a successful *Down!* or *Sit!* and take the dog off the table. If a dog won't comply, or takes so long that it's using up class time, instruct the handler to do some homework.

Send to Table 🐾

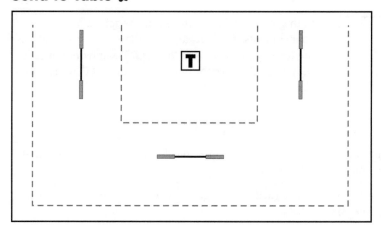

The objective of this exercise is to instill in the dogs a positive attraction for the table. Don't require the dogs to *Sit!* or *Down!* on the table.

Before you start, collect a handful of treats from each student. Your job is to be the baitmaster. You'll stand at the table and load it up with goodies that will inspire the dogs to want to be on the table. Make sure that you're ready to snatch the treat away if a dog refuses to get up on the table and tries to grab the treat from the side.

Divide your students into three small groups. Have each group line up behind one of the three jumps on the approach to the table. The dogs should have a short tab leash attached to their collars. Each line will alternate sending a dog to the table. This allows you to move along very quickly so that you can get in more repetitions.

Around the table is a "fudge line". A second fudge line is drawn outside the group of obstacles. Use surveyor's tape or string to mark the lines (or duct tape if you're indoors). You can tack down the line with golf tees.

1. Start by having each handler trot his dog up to the table and then put the dog up on it; whereupon the baitmaster gives the dog a treat. After the dog gets the treat, the handler releases the dog from the table. Some dogs may want to further inspect the table for the promise of more treats—don't allow them to linger. The handler should use the tab leash to remove the dog from the table, if necessary.

2. Starting behind the first line, each student sends his dog to the table. If a dog is reluctant to leave its handler, then the handler needs to move to the table with the dog. Stay with that dog and handler for a moment and have them try again (and once or twice more) until the dog goes away from the handler from the fudge line to get the treat on the table. Repeat this step several times with all dogs.

3. Now start each dog behind one of the jumps. The handler runs with the dog as it performs the jump, advances with the dog to the first fudge line, and then sends the dog on to the table from there. Repeat this step several times with all dogs.

4. Starting behind the second fudge line, each student sends his dog over the jump and on to the table. This time the handler remains behind the second fudge line. If the dog is reluctant to leave its handler, the handler should move to the first fudge line (or all the way to the table, if necessary). Stay with that dog and handler for a moment to try to work backwards and build the dog's confidence to go away to the table. Repeat this step several times with all dogs.

Set 2

Your set consists of three exercises that use three separate groups of equipment. No equipment movement is required. You may want to consider alternating among the three exercises with each repetition so that you cycle neatly around and have a balanced breaking point when it's time to send your students to the next set.

The weave poles are attached to this set as an independent obstacle. Instruct your students to put their dogs through the weave poles on their own after each repetition of any of the following exercises. Make sure that you read "About the Weave Poles" on page 17.

You'll be introducing a new obstacle to your students—the spread hurdle. Please refer to page 110 in the Appendix for a discussion of the height and depth at which the bars need to be set.

You'll be working with contact obstacles in your set. Remember that your students should reward their dogs only in the contact zone of the descent ramps. The dog is not permitted to leave the contact zone without a quiet release from his handler. If the dog bails off early, he should be picked up and placed back on the contact zone.

Spread Hurdle and A-Frame

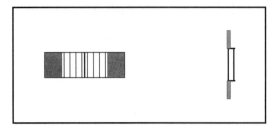

In this set, you will first introduce the spread hurdle to your students. The spread hurdle should be set so that it is not terribly challenging to the dogs. The intention here is simply to introduce the dogs to the concept that there may be a depth dimension to a jump.

1. Each handler leaves the dog in a sit-stay, calls the dog over the jump, and then praises and treats the dog.

2. Side-by-side in a running start with the dog on his left, each handler gives the dog a command to jump and then praises and treats the dog on the other side of the jump.

3. Side-by-side in a running start with the dog on his right, each handler gives the dog a command to jump and then praises and treats the dog on the other side of the jump.

   Now add the A-frame after the spread jump. The instructor should act as baitmaster and place a food tidbit in the down contact zone. Remind your students that the dog should not leave the contact zone without a quiet release from the handler.

4. Side-by-side in a running start with the dog on his left, each handler performs the spread jump and then the A-frame. The handler allows the dog to get the treat in the down contact and then quietly releases him.

5. Side-by-side in a running start with the dog on his right, each handler performs the spread jump and then the A-frame. The handler allows the dog to get the treat in the down contact and then quietly releases him.

6. Repeat steps 4 and 5 several times.

Remind your students to put their dogs through the weave poles after each repetition of this exercise.

Tire and See-Saw

Your students are still learning the see-saw. Therefore, you will first do the tire by itself before including the see-saw in a sequence.

1. Each handler leaves his dog in a sit-stay, calls the dog through the tire, and then praises and treats the dog.

2. Side-by-side in a running start with the dog on his left, each handler gives the dog a command to jump through the tire and then praises and treats the dog on the other side.

3. Side-by-side in a running start with the dog on his right, each handler gives the dog a command to jump through the tire and then praises and treats the dog on the other side.

   Now add the see-saw after the tire. Remind your students to have a food treat in hand, ready to give the dog in the down contact zone of the see-saw.

4. Each handler leaves his dog in a sit-stay and then calls the dog through the tire. The handler praises the dog briefly and then directs the dog onto the see-saw. The instructor should act as a spotter and control the tip of the board from behind the dog. Make sure that the handler treats the dog in the down contact zone and then quietly releases him from the obstacle. Repeat this step several times.

Remind your students to put their dogs through the weave poles after each repetition of this exercise.

Collapsed Tunnel and Dogwalk

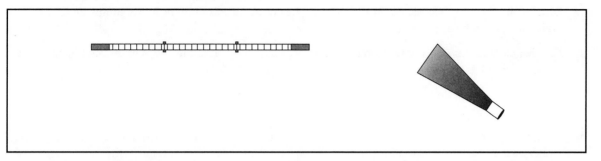

Your students are still learning the collapsed tunnel. Therefore, you will first do the collapsed tunnel by itself.

1. Side-by-side in a running start with the dog on his left, each handler gives the dog a command to do the tunnel and then praises and treats the dog at the exit.

2. Side-by-side in a running start with the dog on his right, each handler gives the dog a command to do the tunnel and then praises and treats the dog at the exit.

   Now add the dogwalk after the tunnel. The instructor should act as a baitmaster and put a food treat in the down contact zone of the dogwalk for each dog. Remind your students that the dog should not leave the contact zone without a quiet release from the handler.

3. Side-by-side in a running start with the dog on his left, each handler performs the collapsed tunnel and the dogwalk. The handler allows the dog to get the treat in the down contact and then quietly releases him.

4. Side-by-side in a running start with the dog on his right, each handler performs the collapsed tunnel and the dogwalk. The handler allows the dog to get the treat in the down contact and then quietly releases him.

5. Repeat steps 3 and 4 several times.

Remind your students to put their dogs through the weave poles after each repetition of this exercise.

Set 3

In this set, you have two jumping exercises that use the same equipment. However, frequent equipment movement will be required during class. Brief your students immediately that they will be moving the equipment between the exercises. You will lay the jump bars on the ground to indicate where to position jumps. Instruct your students to move the jump standards into place.

The jumps should be set at 6" for small dogs and at 12" for big dogs. These exercises are not about jumping for height. Rather, you are interested in control and the dog's attention to his handler.

Simple Sequencing

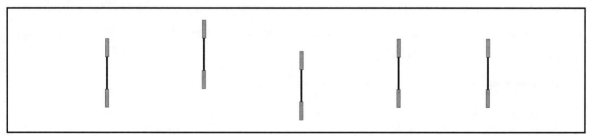

We have two essential objectives in this exercise:

1. Teach the dogs to perform a sequence of obstacles.

2. Teach the dogs to look to their handlers for permission to perform the next obstacle in a sequence.

This exercise is performed with the dog *at the handler's side* (either the left or right). Do *not* allow a lead-out.

1. Each handler puts his dog over the first jump, calls the dog to *Come!* out of the line of jumps, and then praises and treats the dog.

2. Each handler puts his dog over two jumps, calls the dog to *Come!* out of the line of jumps, and then praises and treats the dog.

3. Each handler puts his dog over three jumps, calls the dog to *Come!* out of the line of jumps, and then praises and treats the dog.

4. Each handler puts his dog over four jumps, calls the dog to *Come!* out of the line of jumps, and then praises and treats the dog.

5. Each handler puts his dog over all five jumps, calls the dog to *Come!*, and then praises and treats the dog.

NOTE: If the dog fails to recall out of the line of jumps and takes a subsequent jump, advise the handler to turn around and walk the other way. Avoid making a correction—especially an emotional correction. Have the handler try to hang back farther to influence the dog's turn and also have him put more emphasis on the *Come!* command. The handler may need to work on the *Come!* command as a homework assignment.

Speed Circle

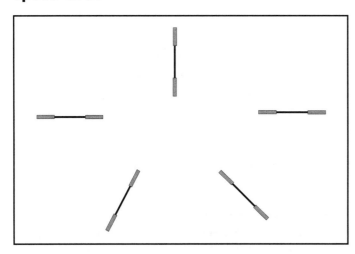

The "Speed Circle" exercise is a sequence that you should do nearly every week in an intermediate program. The purpose of the exercise is to build speed and enthusiasm in the dog.

The handler will take the inside position and consequently run the shorter path.

Remind your students to have treats ready in hand.

Run the sequence in a clockwise direction so that the dog is on the heel-side.

Each dog and handler will do *all* of the following steps *before* the next dog and handler in line work the exercise:

1. With the dog at heel-side, the handler puts the dog over one jump, and then praises and treats the dog.

2. With the dog at heel-side, the handler puts the dog over two jumps, and then praises and treats the dog.

3. With the dog at heel-side, the handler puts the dog over three jumps, and then praises and treats the dog.

4. With the dog at heel-side, the handler puts the dog over four jumps, and then praises and treats the dog.

5. With the dog at heel-side, the handler puts the dog over all five jumps, and then praises and treats the dog.

6. Repeat steps 1–5 with the next dog in line.

During each repetition, work with your students on all of the following:

- Challenge your students to work closer and closer to the center of the circle, if they can. This means that the dog will have to hurry faster to do the circle of jumps. Not all dogs will be comfortable working away from their handlers. It is *not* failure if the dog will not work away at this early moment in their agility training.

- Remind your students to always keep their bodies rotated in the direction of the flow of the sequence.

- Remind your students to use *Come!* if the dog wants to take a straight line rather than continuing the turning in the sequence.

Week 1: Student Notes

Your dog works for you because he trusts you. If you never give your dog any reason to distrust you, he will do almost anything you ask because he *knows* that he can trust you. You're like an infallible god. He knows you would not ask him to do anything that would cause pain. He knows you won't get angry and unreasonable if he doesn't *get it* immediately. He's your pal. He trusts you completely.

Artist: Valerie Pietraszewska

Your dog's unflinching trust is a terrible responsibility. You can nurture that trust only by being trustworthy. If you once fail your dog in this matter of trust, you will plant a permanent seed of doubt in your dog's mind. If you once terrify your dog or allow him to be hurt, then he will never completely trust you again.

It's easy to be an upbeat trainer. You don't hit your dog. You don't belabor your dog with emotional corrections. So, what can go wrong? What can you do to betray your dog's trust?

It's that old devil ego. You've trained this fine working animal. You know the heights your dog is capable of jumping. You know his powers of scaling, and weaving, and his willingness to dive into the unknown. And you are aware that because of your working relationship, your dog will do all of this at your bidding.

There have been a variety of injuries to dogs trained in the sport of agility when they are asked to hurdle or scale objects in the world which were not designed for the sport; but merely have common dimensions with some agility obstacles. Here is a list of "Things that are not agility obstacles". As you read this list, use your imagination to figure out what might go wrong if these things are used as agility obstacles.

These are *NOT* hurdles	These are *NOT* dogwalks	These are *NOT* pipe tunnels
Cyclone fences	Stone walls	Drainage pipes
Stone walls	Playground monkey bars	Caves in the wild
Stone or iron park benches	Scrap wood piles	Crawl spaces
Cemetery headstones	Fallen trees	Culverts
Guard rails	Narrow cliff ledges	
Wrought iron fences	Bleachers	

Sending Your Dog to Work

This week in class you did an exercise designed to put some distance between you and your dog. At the center of the exercise was a table, and you worked at sending your dog to the table from progressively greater distances. You can do an exercise like this in your own backyard. You might not have a table to work with, but a jump or a children's play tunnel from a toy store (about $20) will do just as well.

SAFETY NOTE: When you put a bend in a pipe tunnel, you must somehow secure the tunnel so that it doesn't straighten when the dog goes through. However, be careful of using bricks or other hard or sharp objects which might injure your dog if he collides with them while passing through the tunnel.

The illustrations that follow show you how to begin the process. In this exercise, you'll not only be sending the dog away from you to work, you'll also be calling the dog back to you. This is just as important as the dog's willingness to go away to perform the jump.

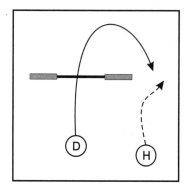

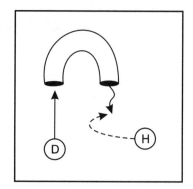

If you are using a jump, begin by approaching the jump with your dog as shown in the illustration on the left. Then call your dog back to you, praise him, and give him a treat.

If you are using a tunnel, put a bend in the tunnel so that your dog comes straight back to you as shown in the illustration on the right. Meet your dog at the tunnel exit, praise him, and give him a treat.

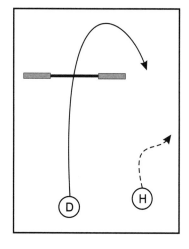

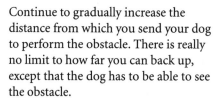

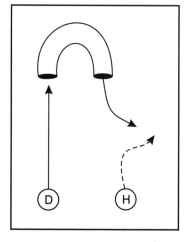

As your dog gets the idea that all he has to do for praise and a treat is to *go* and do the obstacle, gradually start to back up as shown in the illustation on the left and the one on the right.

If your dog turns back to you and fails to go all the way to the obstacle, you should do two things:

1. Withhold the dog's reward—the dog does not get praise or a treat. Don't get angry or correct the dog.

2. Start closer to the obstacle and slowly work back out again.

Continue to gradually increase the distance from which you send your dog to perform the obstacle. There is really no limit to how far you can back up, except that the dog has to be able to see the obstacle.

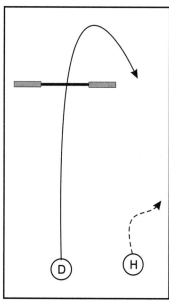

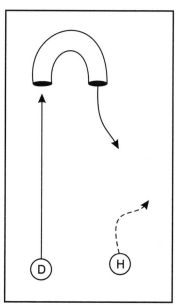

After the dog performs the jump or tunnel, move forward slightly and step out to the side to call the dog away from the obstacle as shown in these two illustrations. If you're using a jump, do *not* allow the dog to come back over the jump (called a back-jump). It might look cute or you may even think it's desirable for the dog to volunteer to do an obstacle; but it's neither cute, nor desirable. One of your objectives is for the dog to do an obstacle *only* when you direct him to do so.

Week 2: Instructor Notes

Artist: Nancy Krouse-Culley

Come! is the most powerful command in agility. It can be used to redirect the dog from one path to another. In fact, a handler could effectively work an entire course without earning an off-course using only a *Come!* command. However, many dogs do not respond promptly when called. Sometimes this is because of a lack of training, but it's also often caused by inappropriate application of the *Come!* command. A common training mistake is to call the dog to punish him for some misdeed or to do something that the dog perceives as unpleasant (such as bathing him or trimming his nails). The dog then associates getting punished or having something unpleasant happen to him with the owner calling him to *Come!*.

You see the results of this inappropriate application of the command all the time in agility. When a course calls for a change of direction, especially in a 180° turn, the handler says *Come!* and the dog slows down, tucks his tail between his legs, and slinks back toward his handler. This means that in training if the dog is being called to turn back, he is expecting to be punished or reprimanded.

A good instructor will spot the very moment that a handler calls his dog to be chastised or reprimanded. The instructor should explain to the handler that he is asking for performance problems. Remind handlers that whenever they call their dogs, it should be a positive experience so that the dogs *want* to come. If for some reason it is truly necessary to reprimand the dog, the handler needs to go and get the dog; *not* call the dog to him. Also watch for handlers who make the mistake of calling their dogs three or four times before the dog responds—*Fluffy Come! Come, Fluffy, Come! Fluffy, I said Come!* This only serves to train the dog that it really isn't necessary to respond to the handler until he yells *Come!* for the fourth time.

It doesn't hurt to include regular obedience recalls in your training program. These should be full of praise and treats and positive reinforcement. Also work on agility recall sequences. For example, you can begin with a single jump. Have your students put the dog over the jump, use *Come!* to turn full circle, and then put the dog over the jump again in the same direction. This should be done with a lot of enthusiasm, praise, and treats.

	Set 1	Set 2	Set 3
Week 2	**A.D.D. Tunnel Exercise** **Blind to Spread Hurdle** *Obstacles Required:* pipe tunnel, tire, spread hurdle, collapsed tunnel	**Inside-Out Contacts** **Dogwalk Straightover** *Obstacles Required:* A-frame, winged jump, see-saw, weave poles, dogwalk, table	**Send to Jump** **Speed Circle** **Branching Path** 🐾 *Obstacles Required:* five winged jumps, long jump *Note:* Major equipment movement is required between exercises.

Organizational Notes

Remind your instructors that if an exercise is clearly too advanced for the dogs and handlers, it should be simplified so that everyone can end on a positive note. Also remind all the instructors to mark the Progress Worksheet if any students are having trouble.

Start the training session by doing the control exercise on page 29 with *all* students. Then break into groups for the training sets, if you're going to work multiple sets simultaneously.

NOTE: Set 3 will require major equipment movement between exercises.

Week 2: Progress Worksheet

Instructors: **Date:**

Handler and Dog	Present	Notes

GENERAL NOTES:

Week 2: Facility Layout

One square = 10'

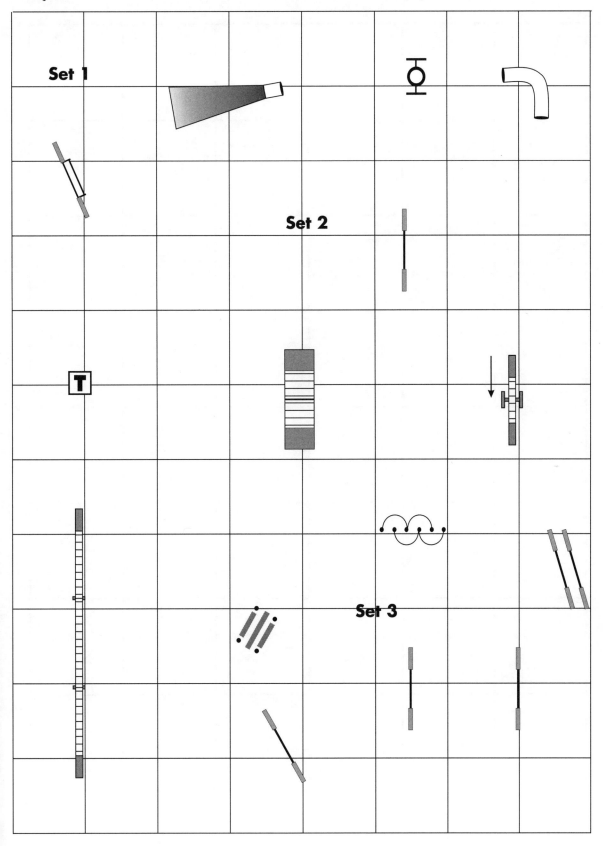

Week 2: Facility Layout Worksheet

Design your Facility Layout using a 1" = 10' scale (standard agility template)

Week 2: Exercises

Start the class by doing the control exercise with everyone. Then break into smaller groups if you're going to work the training sets simultaneously.

Control Exercise

Start the class with an obedience warm-up exercise. Dogs will work *off-lead.*

- Have your students free heel their dogs into the field of equipment. Don't work in a line—allow them to go where they will. Allow the dogs to sniff and to inspect the equipment, but keep the dogs off the equipment.

- Heel the dogs at attention into a long line. You need 8' to 10' between the dogs.

- *Down!* the dogs. Instruct handlers to leave their dogs and walk about 15', forming a line facing the dogs.

- Wait about 30 seconds (the instructor should keep time). If any dog breaks its stay during this time, the handler will collect the dog and hold on to it for the remainder of the exercise.

- Recall the dogs *one* at a time. Each handler commands his dog to *Come!*. With any luck, the right dog will get up and come directly to the handler. If the dog does not do so, the handler will go and collect his dog. If the wrong dog comes, that dog's handler will collect his dog and put him back in a down with the other dogs.

End of exercise. If any dogs are *not* coming to the handler, demonstrate how to teach *Come!* using a long line and food and praise. Mark your worksheets for dogs having difficulty with control.

Set 1

Your set consists of two exercises that use the same equipment. No equipment movement will be required. You'll be using the spread hurdle. Please refer to page 110 in the Appendix for a discussion of the height and depth at which the bars need to be set.

A.D.D. Tunnel Exercise

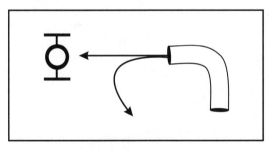

The purpose of this exercise is to reinforce the dog's "job" in tunnel performance and to teach the dog to be aware of the handler's signal when performing a sequence. This is also an opportunity to work on *Come!*. First you will work only with the pipe tunnel. Then you will add the tire.

1. With the dog on his right, each handler puts the dog in the tunnel, runs to meet the dog as it emerges from the tunnel, and then praises and treats the dog.

2. With the dog on his right, each handler puts the dog in the tunnel and runs forward only half the length of the tunnel. As the dog emerges from the tunnel, the handler calls the dog to *Come!* and then praises and treats the dog.

3. With the dog on his right, each handler puts the dog in the tunnel and does not move forward at all. As the dog emerges from the tunnel, the handler calls the dog to *Come!* and then praises and treats the dog.

   Now add the tire to the exercise.

4. With the dog on his right, each handler puts the dog in the tunnel. The handler meets the dog as it emerges from the tunnel and then pushes the dog out to do the tire jump, using a good hand signal and a *Tire!* command. Make sure that the handler praises and treats the dog after the tire.

5. Alternately repeat steps 3 and 4 several times.

Blind to Spread Hurdle

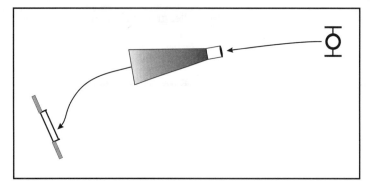

The purpose of this exercise is to allow the handler to work on the *Come!* command with his dog, and to allow the dogs to do some simple sequencing.

This early in their agility careers, many dogs will still be timid of the collapsed tunnel. Consequently, the instructor should pick up the chute for timid dogs allowing them to see daylight.

Do *not* permit the handler to lead out. The handler will begin with his dog on his right side.

Remind your students to have a food treat ready in hand. It is important that your students reward their dogs quickly and not be fishing around in a baggie for a treat while the dog is waiting. While a prompt reward is always important in order for the dog to associate the treat with a correct performance, timeliness of reward is particularly important when you are calling the dogs out of the sequence. Turning away from an obstacle and coming back to the handler—especially for a dog that really wants to perform the next obstacle in sequence—must always be a positive experience.

1. Each handler puts the dog through the tire. The handler should turn *away* from the sequence, call his dog to *Come!*, and then reward the dog with praise and a treat.

2. Each handler puts the dog through the tire and then through the collapsed tunnel. The handler should turn *away* from the sequence, call his dog to *Come!*, and then reward the dog with praise and a treat.

3. Now each handler does all three obstacles in the sequence. Challenge your students to do a bit of crafty handling in this set. Many dogs will slow down in the collapsed tunnel. The handler should *not* wait for the dog. Instead, the handler should sprint ahead so he gets a good lead; then as the dog exits the collapsed tunnel, he can call the dog over the spread hurdle. Remind your students that it's the handler's responsibility to help the dog build up stride for spread hurdles.

4. Repeat steps 1–3 two or three times.

NOTE: If the dog fails to recall away from the sequence and takes the next obstacle, advise the handler to turn around and walk the other way. Avoid making a correction—especially an emotional correction. Have the handler try to hang back further to influence the dog's turn and also have him put more emphasis on the *Come!* command. The handler may need to work on the *Come!* command as a homework assignment.

Set 2

You have two exercises that use two separate sets of equipment. No equipment movement will be required except that you will have to pivot the see-saw during the "Inside-Out Contacts" exercise in order to reverse the sequence.

You'll be working with contact obstacles in your set. Remember that your students should reward their dogs only in the contact zone of the descent ramps. The dog is not permitted to leave the contact zone without a quiet release from his handler. If the dog bails off early he should be picked up and placed back on the contact zone.

NOTE: Some students will object to picking up their dog giving you the excuse, "My dog hates it when I do that!". This is a lame objection. Tell the student that you don't want your dog to like it. It could be that the more distasteful it is to the dog, the faster he will stop bailing off contacts.

Inside-Out Contacts

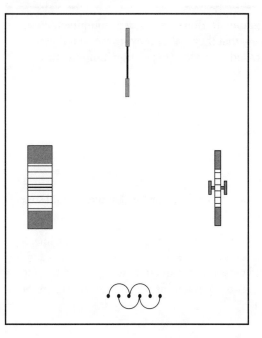

The purpose of this set is to give your students some solid work on contact obstacles.

The instructor will no longer act as baitmaster. Instead, instruct your students to have a treat ready in hand. The dog will be looking for the treat as he comes down the ramp. The handler should pause momentarily, give the dog the treat, and then quietly release the dog from the obstacle.

The weave poles are not actually a part of this sequence. Instruct your students that they should do the weave poles on their own between repetitions of the exercise. Remind them that in Week 5 they will be doing a Weave Pole Knock-out and that they should be getting their weave pole game together. As you work, you might query each group as to how many of them have weave poles set up at home.

1. Each handler works the sequence in a clockwise direction: A-frame–jump–see-saw. Remind your students that their dog is *not* to leave the yellow contact zone until the handler gives a quiet release command.

2. Reverse the sequence and have each handler start with the see-saw. You'll have to turn around the see-saw so that it's going in the right direction. Again, the dog is *not* to leave the contact zone until the handler gives a quiet release command.

NOTES: Remember, if a dog is bailing off the obstacle without getting a release from the handler, instruct the handler to physically pick up the dog and put him back on the contact zone.

Be especially watchful of the handler who is giving his dog a treat and then allowing the dog to pop off the contact before being released. This is not a good training strategy in the long term for the dog.

Dogwalk Straightover

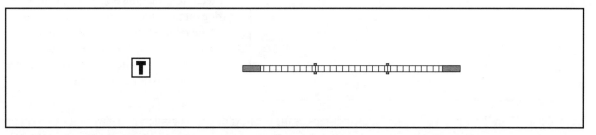

Instruct your students that you will no longer be baiting the contact zone of the dogwalk. Instead, students should have a treat ready in hand so that they can reward the dog when he waits in the contact zone.

1. Each handler performs the dogwalk and then the table. Remind your students that their dog is *not* to leave the yellow contact until the handler gives a quiet release command. You can require either a *Down!* or a *Sit!* on the table. The performance should provide evidence that the dog and handler have been working on these skills at home. It is not very realistic to expect the dog to *Down!* or to *Sit!* by being exposed to the obstacle once a week in class. Use the opportunity to get on the soapbox and urge your students to be working on *Down!* and *Sit!* at home.

2. Now each handler returns over the dogwalk after performing the table. The sequence is: dogwalk–table–dogwalk. Again, the dog is *not* to leave the down contact zone of the dogwalk until the handler gives a quiet release command.

Set 3

In this set, you have three jumping exercises that use the same equipment. However, frequent equipment movement will be required during class. Brief your students immediately that they will be moving the equipment between the exercises. You will lay the jump bars on the ground to indicate where to position jumps. Instruct your students to move the jump standards into place.

Note that the "Branching Path" exercise is a bit advanced. If your students are struggling, specifically with the *Get Out!* command, simplify the exercise so that it ends on a successful and positive note. The exercise can be redesigned so that the handler works only on the side of the required turn.

Send to Jump

Set up a single bar jump and perform the following steps:

1. Each handler in the group puts his dog over the jump. As the dog clears the jump, the handler should step out to the right and call his dog back to him. Praise and treat the dog.

2. Now draw a line 3' away from the jump. Each handler sends his dog over the jump from behind the line. As the dog clears the jump, the handler steps out to the right, calls his dog back to him, and then praises and treats the dog. If the dog refuses the jump, the handler should cross the line and put his dog over the jump. It's important for the handler to step out to the side so that the dog does not turn around and perform the jump again when the handler calls him (called a back-jump).

Speed Circle

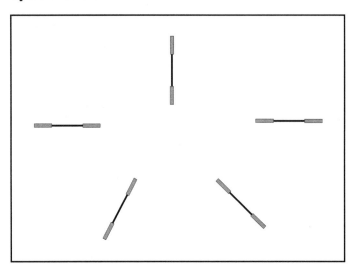

Remember, the purpose of the exercise is to build speed and enthusiasm in the dog.

The handler will take the inside position and consequently run the shorter path.

Remind your students to have treats ready in hand.

Run the sequence in a counterclockwise direction so that the dog is on the off-side (dog on the handler's right). Many dogs will be reluctant to work on the off-side, especially dogs that have been trained in the sport of obedience. Don't let them give up. Persevere with the exercise.

Each dog and handler will do *all* of the following steps *before* the next dog and handler in line work the exercise:

1. With the dog on the off-side, the handler puts the dog over one jump and then praises and treats the dog.

2. With the dog on the off-side, the handler puts the dog over two jumps and then praises and treats the dog.

3. With the dog on the off-side, the handler puts the dog over three jumps and then praises and treats the dog.

4. With the dog on the off-side, the handler puts the dog over four jumps and then praises and treats the dog.

5. With the dog on the off-side, the handler puts the dog over all five jumps and then praises and treats the dog.

6. Repeat steps 1–5 with the next dog in line.

During each repetition of the speed circle exercise, work with your students on all of the following:

- Challenge your students to work closer and closer to the center of the circle, if they can. This means that the dog will have to hurry faster to do the circle of jumps. Not all dogs will be comfortable working away from their handlers. It is *not* failure if the dog will not work away at this early moment in their agility training—particularly if the dog is not yet comfortable working on the off-side.

- Remind your students to always keep their bodies rotated in the direction of the flow of the sequence.

- Remind your students to use *Come!* if the dog wants to take a straight line rather than continuing the turning in the sequence.

Branching Path 🐾

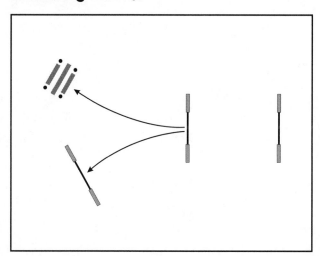

This sequence requires the handler to alternate turning 45° to the left or 45° to the right coming off the down-the-middle flow established by the first two jumps.

You will use two important commands in this sequence—*Come!* and *Get Out!*.

Your students have already been introduced to the *Come!* command. However, you need to pause a moment and explain the *Get Out!* command, which is the opposite of the *Come!* command. With *Come!* you want the dog moving in *toward* you to perform an obstacle. With *Get Out!* you want the dog to veer out laterally *away* from you to perform an obstacle.

It's worth noting that the dogs won't actually learn the command from this exercise. But the rule of 5000 applies here—anything you do 5000 times, you own.

1. With the dog on the handler's left, each handler leaves the dog in a sit-stay. The handler then leads out and calls the dog over the first jump. As the dog commits to the second jump, the handler turns right (an exaggerated turn) and commands the dog to *Come!* and then *Jump!*. Remind the handler that he really needs to step through the long jump so that the dog has plenty of stride to clear the obstacles.

2. With the dog on the handler's left, each handler leaves the dog in a sit-stay. The handler then leads out and calls the dog over the first jump. As the dog commits to the second jump, the handler pushes to the left towards the bar jump (getting in the dog's path in such a way that the dog must veer left) and commands the dog to *Get Out!* and then *Jump!*.

3. With the dog on the handler's right, each handler leaves the dog in a sit-stay. The handler leads out and calls the dog over the first jump. As the dog commits to the second jump, the handler turns left (an exaggerated turn) and commands the dog to *Come!* and then *Jump!*.

4. With the dog on the handler's right, each handler leaves the dog in a sit-stay. The handler leads out and calls the dog over the first jump. As the dog commits to the second jump, the handler pushes to the right towards the long jump (getting in the dog's path in such a way that the dog must veer right) and commands the dog to *Get Out!* and then *Jump!*. Remind the handler that he really needs to step through the long jump so that the dog has plenty of stride to clear the obstacle.

Intermediate Agility Workbook

Week 2: Student Notes

Directional commands play an important role in agility. A **directional command** is a command that is intended to change the direction in which your dog is moving.

You are probably well versed in the use of the *Come!* command since it's a critical command for everyday life with your dog. If this is the case, your dog already knows at least one directional command—*Come!* is the most important directional command used in agility.

Artist: Bud Houston

The next directional command you will start teaching your dog is the *Get Out!* command. *Get Out!* is a directional command that will improve your ability to deal with various course challenges in agility. This command is used when you would like your dog to move *laterally* away from you (either to the left or right), relative to your position. This is not the same as a *Go!* or *Go On!* command, which most handlers use to direct the dog to continue forward along its current path—regardless of the handler's position.

First Steps: *Get Out!*

The following is a simple exercise that you can practice in the house with your Lazy Boy™ recliner to help your dog better understand the *Get Out!* command.

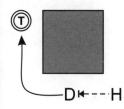

1. Begin with the dog on-lead in heel position. You and the dog should be facing a large obstruction (such as a chair or recliner) that restricts forward movement.

2. Place a toy or treat placed beyond the obstruction (out of the dog's sight) as shown in the illustration.

3. Command *Get Out!* and step into the dog with your left foot. Using your left hand, push laterally away from your body to encourage dog to move away sideways and to the left.

4. If the dog complies, allow him to get the reward. If not, use the leash to guide dog and show him exactly what you what him to do.

5. Repeat steps 1 through 4 until the dog gets up and moves laterally on the verbal *Get Out!* command alone; in other words, you no longer have to step into the dog in order for him to get up and move. Then try the exercise off-lead.

6. Now repeat all the steps starting with the dog on your right side as shown in the second illustration.

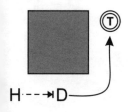

NOTE: Working with the dog on your right may feel very uncomfortable for both you and the dog. However, it's important for your agility training that both of you get used to working this way. So be patient and persevere. Be prepared for your dog to take longer to figure out this variation of the exercise than he did when he started on your left side.

Come! and *Get Out!*

You can practice using *Come!* and *Get Out!* in your backyard with this simple sequence. Only three obstacles are required. For the purpose of illustration, we'll use three jumps. However, you could just as well use two jumps and a tunnel, a tire and a jump and a tunnel, and so on.

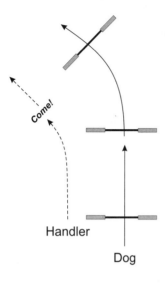

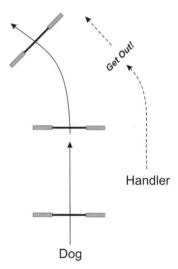

To start with, put yourself on the side in the direction that the dog will turn as shown in the illustration on the left. After the first two jumps, command *Come!* in a clear voice and turn sharply left to give the dog an additional clue to the change of direction. You should give your dog enthusiastic praise when he goes over the jump, to demonstrate how happy and excited you are by his work. Give him a bite of his favorite food treat.

In the next variation of the exercise, you should start on the side *opposite* of the direction the dog will turn as shown in the illustration on the right. Notice that we're giving the handler (who is most likely slower than his dog) a slight lead-out advantage. After the first two jumps, command *Get Out!* in a clear voice and veer sharply left, encroaching in your dog's path, to give the dog an additional clue to the change of direction. Again, praise and give your dog a treat for successful performance of the exercise.

Those Darned Weave Poles

So, how is it going with the weave poles? You should certainly have a set of weave poles set up in the yard by now. If your dog is still having difficulty with the poles, you should try using a good dose of dinner-time psychology.

Dinner-time psychology is the ultimate in motivation for most dogs—the dog will get his dinner based on his performance of the weave poles. Divide your dog's dinner into four parts. Give the dog one part each time he does the weave poles for you.

Keep in mind that learning can be stressful for your dog. Don't require your dog to weave for hours every day. About five minutes one or twice a day should be enough. Always try to end on a positive note.

If your dog is failing more often than he is having success, you are doing something wrong. Talk to your instructor to get some ideas about changing your at-home training program. It's up to you to help your dog have success.

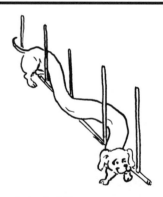

Artist: Jaci Cotton

Week 3: Instructor Notes

The wise, old agility instructor sometimes has to teach both people and dogs some very simple lessons about behavior that are possibly out of the scope of agility training.

Have you ever seen a five-year-old in a grocery store who needed an alpha correction? Sure you have, but you probably hesitated to do so because a parent or two wouldn't appreciate you giving their child a much needed lesson in manners and discipline. If they had a clue that it was necessary, they would probably do it themselves.

As an agility instructor, however, you can probably be more free with people's dogs than you might be with their children. However, you are really obligated to teach both the dog *and* the dog's handler, if the lesson is to be effective.

Artist: Nancy Krouse-Culley

Take, for instance, the dog that likes to jump up on your chest. There are a couple of pretty good corrections for this behavior, but both have to be fairly automatic so that the dog immediately associates his own action with what happens to him. Many behavior books recommend the knee in the chest so that you push the dog off and backwards. This is often effective and it's easy to teach even to the clueless handler.

However, when a dog jumps up in my chest I take it pretty personally. I like to use a quick and effective response that I once saw a breeder do. Bop that silly dog right on the nose with the heel of your hand and say *Off!* as you make the correction. You can do it right in stride while having a conversation with the handler.

	Set 1	Set 2	Set 3
Week 3	**Double and Tunnel Looping Sequence** 🐾 *Obstacles Required:* pipe tunnel, tire, collapsed tunnel, see-saw, two winged jumps	**Can Your Dog Really Weave?** 🐾 **Over and Back** *Obstacles Required:* weave poles, table, spread jump, long jump, one winged jump, dogwalk, pipe tunnel	**Send to Jump** **Speed Circle** **Options** 🐾 *Obstacles Required:* five winged jumps, A-frame *Note:* Major equipment movement is required between exercises.

Organizational Notes

Talk to your instructors about monitoring their students for an upbeat attitude. If a dog is struggling, it is up to the instructors to make sure that the handler does not get angry or impatient with the dog. Keep in mind that an instructor's most important job is to help build confidence and enthusiasm in both dogs and handlers.

Remind all the instructors to mark the Progress Worksheet if any students are having trouble.

Start the training session by doing the control exercise on page 41 with *all* students. Then break into groups for the training sets, if you're going to work multiple sets simultaneously.

NOTE: Set 3 will require major equipment movement between exercises.

Week 3: Progress Worksheet

Instructors: **Date:**

Handler and Dog	Present	Notes

GENERAL NOTES:

Week 3: Facility Layout

One square = 10'

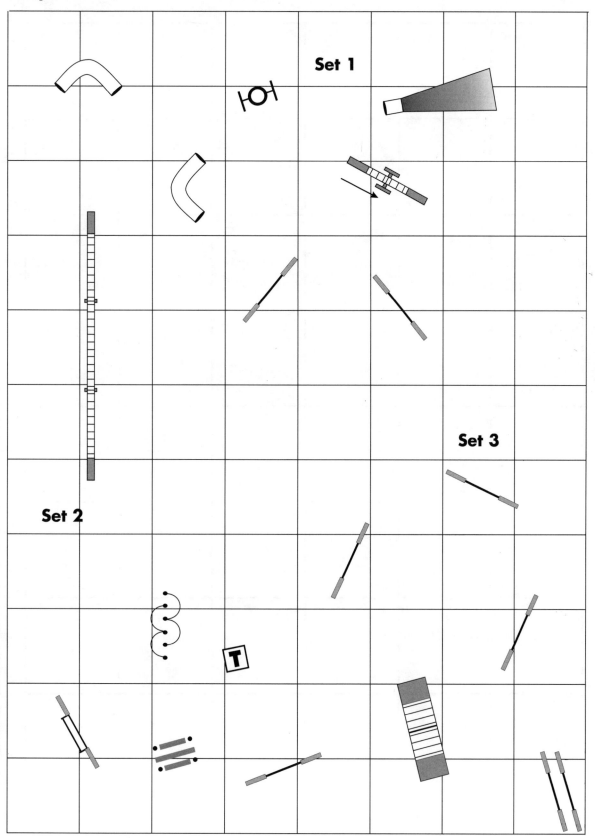

Week 3: Facility Layout Worksheet

Design your Facility Layout using a 1" = 10' scale (standard agility template)

Week 3: Exercises

Start the class by doing the control exercise with everyone. Then break into smaller groups if you're going to work the training sets simultaneously.

Control Exercise

Start the class with an obedience warm-up exercise. Dogs will work *off-lead*.

- Have your students free heel their dogs into the field of equipment. Don't work in a line—allow them to go where they will. Allow the dogs to sniff and to inspect the equipment, but keep the dogs off the equipment.

- Heel the dogs at attention into a long line. You need 8' to 10' between the dogs.

- *Sit!* the dogs. Instruct handlers to leave their dogs and walk about 15', forming a line facing the dogs.

- Wait about 30 seconds (the instructor should keep time). If any dog breaks its stay during this time, the handler will collect the dog and hold on to it for the remainder of the exercise.

- Recall the dogs *one* at a time. Each handler commands his dog to *Come!* With any luck, the right dog will get up and come directly to the handler. If the dog does not do so, the handler will go and collect his dog. If the wrong dog comes, that dog's handler will collect his dog and put him back in a down with the other dogs.

End of exercise. Mark your worksheets for dogs having difficulty with control.

Set 1

Your set consists of two exercises that use the same equipment. No equipment movement will be required.

Note that the "Looping Sequence" exercise is a bit advanced. If your students are struggling, simplify the exercise so that it ends on a successful and positive note. The exercise can be redesigned to be a simple circle. Arrange the see-saw and collapsed tunnel to be performed in a clockwise direction to simplify the exercise so that your students can work their dogs on the heel-side. Arrange the set so that it can be worked in a counterclockwise direction for slightly more advanced work, since the dogs will have to work on the handler's off-side, or non-obedience side.

You'll be working with contact obstacles in your set. Remember that your students should reward their dogs only in the contact zone of the descent ramps. The dog is not permitted to leave the contact zone without a quiet release from his handler. If the dog bails off early he should be picked up and placed back on the contact zone.

Double and Tunnel

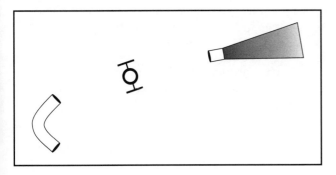

The purpose of this exercise is to do some simple sequencing with the dogs: pipe tunnel–tire–collapsed tunnel. By this time, most of the dogs in your intermediate class should be plunging into the collapsed tunnel readily. This set adds speed to the tunnel. Your students should be hurrying to the collapsed tunnel and giving a good signal.

What is a good signal? A hand out to the left isn't everything. Your dog already knows what side he's on. Use the left hand to motion towards the tunnel. The handler should be rushing up on the tunnel and pointing into it, saying *Tunnel!* or *Get In!* or whatever their command for the obstacle is. Of course, the handler needs to do this without actually stopping. If the handler stops in front of the tunnel, the dog is likely to stop. The dog needs to have a sense that the handler is going on and so should he (the dog).

It's time to talk to your students about variable food reward for correct performance. If a dog understands the desired performance and does it, there comes a time when he really shouldn't get a treat with every correct performance. This keeps the dog interested and possibly working harder.

- In the first repetition of this exercise, the handlers should give their dogs a food treat.

- After that, however, withhold the treat every other repetition. But just because you don't use a food reward does not mean that there should be no reward at all—remind your students to give the dogs praise to tell them they did the job right.

- For each repetition of this exercise, allow your students to work their dogs on either side, or to lead out.

Looping Sequence 🐾

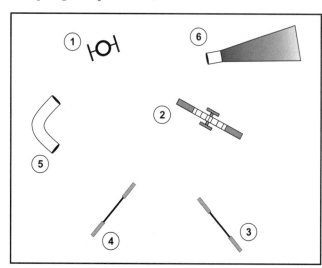

The purpose of this exercise is to motivate the dogs (and the handlers) to work a smooth flowing sequence.

Your students will see that the sequence has an advanced technical feature; that is, the path of the sequence crosses itself—as the dog and handler move from one tunnel to the other tunnel, they will cross their original path from the tire to the see-saw.

The instructor should be aware of any dogs that are having difficulty with the see-saw. Be prepared to work as a spotter on the see-saw and control the board from the behind the dog so that the board tips under control.

1. Allow your students to walk the sequence, without their dogs, so that they can think through what they have to do as handlers to get their dogs to perform the sequence smoothly.

2. Each handler runs the entire sequence with two control breaks—one break after the see-saw and one after the pipe tunnel—where the handler will stop, praise the dog, and give the dog a treat before continuing on.

3. Each handler runs the entire sequence with one control break after the see-saw.

4. Each handler runs the sequence without breaks.

When you run the sequence without control breaks, keep the following in mind:

- Running a sequence without breaks does *not* mean that you will forego requiring the dog to stop in the see-saw down contact until released by his handler. Nor does it mean that the handler should forget little details like using *Come!* to help guide the dog through this set, which has a constantly changing direction of flow.

- This sequence has six obstacles, so many handlers will want to hurry and show how fast and furious they can move. That's okay. But *you* need to have an eye for the dog. Is the dog equally motivated to be working fast and furious? If so, fine—just as long as they do the exercise under control.

Intermediate Agility Workbook

Set 2

Your set consists of two exercises that use separate sets of equipment. No equipment movement will be required between exercises. You'll be using the spread hurdle. Please refer to page 110 in the Appendix for a discussion of the height and depth at which the bars need to be set.

Note that the "Can Your Dog Really Weave?" exercise is a bit advanced. If your students are struggling, simplify the exercise so that it ends on a successful and positive note. The exercise can be redesigned so that the obstacles are arranged in a simple circle.

You'll be working with contact obstacles in your set. Remember that your students should reward their dogs only in the contact zone of the descent ramps. The dog is not permitted to leave the contact zone without a quiet release from his handler. If the dog bails off early he should be picked up and placed back on the contact zone.

Can Your Dog Really Weave? 🐾

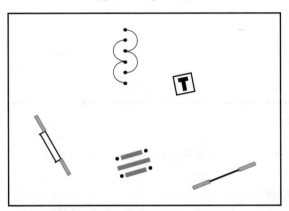

This exercise consists of two separate sequences. In the first sequence, your students will perform only the spread hurdle and the weave poles.

1. Each handler leaves his dog on a sit-stay behind the spread hurdle, takes a lead-out past the spread hurdle, and calls the dog over the jump. The handler praises the dog and then turns and performs the weave poles. Repeat this steps once or twice and then proceed to the second sequence.

2. Each handler performs: spread hurdle–table–bar jump–long jump–weave poles.

In this second sequence, your students will for the first time execute a 180° turn. This is a good opportunity to get your students to do some of their own problem solving. First show your students the sequence they are going to run. Then explain to them that their dogs will have to turn 180° from the bar jump to the long jump. You should also point out that their dogs should be in a down position on the table and that you will be counting while the dog is on the table.

Run the set and allow your students to handle it as they feel it will work best for them. Now, your student's ability to solve this puzzle might surprise you. But the number of solutions for making the 180° turn from the bar jump to the long jump is fairly finite. These are the possible solutions:

- If the dog has a reliable *Stay!* on the table, the handler will be tempted to lead out past the jump. This would allow the handler to turn the dog around and plunge back over the long jump towards the weave poles. The problem with this strategy is that the dog is likely to get too far ahead of the handler on the approach to the weave poles, making for an off-course or a very ugly entry to the poles.

- If the dog has a reliable *Come!*, the handler will likely run with the dog as he performs the jump and rely on a *Come!* command to turn the dog to the long jump. This handler can play the inside of the loop and be in good control for the entry to the poles. The only downside of this strategy is that the dog might take a long or hesitant loop as it reverses direction after the jump.

- If the dog has a reliable send, the handler will be able to push the dog over the jump and get a lead in front of the dog as the dog executes the 180° turn. This puts the handler in front of the long jump, which will help encourage speed over the long jump and also allow the handler to neatly manage the entry to the weave poles. This is a very advanced maneuver and shows a handler who is doing work at home between classes.

After your students work this sequence several times. Take the time to point out the different solutions you saw. In subsequent repetitions, you could challenge them to try a strategy other than the one they initially elected.

Over and Back

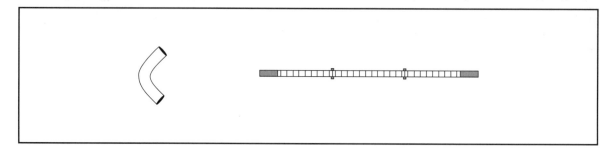

Instruct your students to have a treat ready in hand so that they can reward the dog when he waits in the contact.

1. Each handler performs the dogwalk and then the tunnel (either end). Remind your students that their dog is *not* to leave the yellow contact until the handler gives a quiet release command.

2. Now have each handler return over the dogwalk after performing the tunnel. The sequence will be dogwalk–tunnel–dogwalk. Again, the dog is *not* to leave the contact until the handler gives a quiet release command.

Set 3

In this set, you have three jumping exercises that share some of the same equipment. Frequent equipment movement will be required during class. Brief your students immediately that they will be moving the equipment between the exercises. You will lay the jump bars on the ground to indicate where to position jumps. Instruct your students to move the jump standards into place.

Note that the "Options" exercise is a bit advanced. If your students are struggling with the *Get Out!* command, simplify the exercise so that it ends on a successful and positive note. The exercise can be redesigned so that the handler works only on the side of the required turn.

You'll be working with contact obstacles in your set. Remember that your students should reward their dogs only in the contact zone of the descent ramps. The dog is not permitted to leave the contact zone without a quiet release from his handler. If the dog bails off early he should be picked up and placed back on the contact zone.

Send to Jump

Set up a single bar jump and perform the following steps:

1. Each handler in the group puts his dog over the jump. As the dog clears the jump, the handler steps out to the right, calls his dog back to him, and then praises and treats the dog.

2. Now draw a line 5' away from the jump. Each handler sends the dog over the jump from behind the line. As the dog clears the jump, the handler steps out to the right, calls his dog back to him, and then praises and treats the dog. If the dog refuses the jump, the handler should cross the line and put his dog over the jump. It's important for the handler to step out to the side so that the dog does not turn around and perform the jump again when the handler calls him (called a back-jump).

Speed Circle

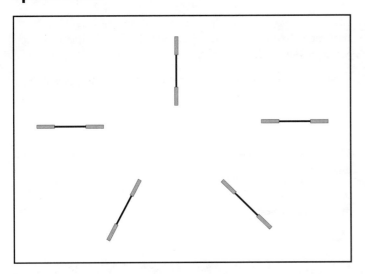

Remember, the purpose of the exercise is to build speed and enthusiasm in the dog.

The handler will take the inside position and consequently run the shorter path.

Remind your students to have treats ready in hand.

First run the sequence in a clockwise manner and then run it in a counterclockwise direction, so that dogs will have an opportunity to work on both sides of the handler.

Each dog and handler will do *all* of the following steps *before* the next dog and handler in line work the exercise:

1. With the dog at heel-side, the handler puts the dog over two jumps and then praises and treats the dog.

2. With the dog on the off-side, the handler puts the dog over two jumps and the praises and treats the dog.

3. With the dog at heel-side, the handler puts the dog over four jumps and then praises and treats the dog.

4. With the dog on the off-side, the handler puts the dog over four jumps and then praises and treats the dog.

5. With the dog at heel-side, the handler puts the dog over six jumps and then praises and treats the dog.

6. With the dog on the off-side, the handler puts the dog over six jumps and then praises and treats the dog.

7. Repeat steps 1–6 with the next dog in line.

During each repetition of the speed circle exercise, work with your students on all of the following:

- Challenge your students to work closer and closer to the center of the circle, if they can. This means that the dog will have to hurry faster to do the circle of jumps. Not all dogs will be comfortable working away from their handlers. It is *not* failure if the dog will not work away at this early moment in their agility training—particularly if the dog is not yet comfortable working on the off-side.

- Remind your students to always keep their bodies rotated in the direction of the flow of the sequence.

- Remind your students to use *Come!* if the dog wants to take a straight line rather than continuing the turning in the sequence.

Options 🐾

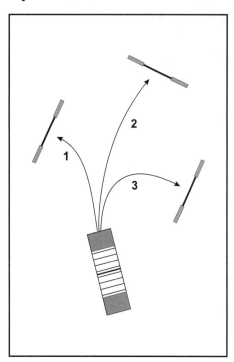

For the first time, you will pose a complex handling challenge after the A-frame. In this exercise, you will alternate the finishing jump the dogs take after the A-frame.

However, performance of the A-frame is the most important task. The handlers should have a treat in hand to reward the dog in the contact zone. The dog should not leave the contact zone without a quiet release from the handler.

Allow your students to start on whichever side of the A-frame they want.

Each of the three paths your students will try is going to present them with a different challenge:

• Path 1 over the jump on the left is the most direct.

• Path 2 over the center jump requires a subtle turn to the right.

• Path 3 over the jump on the right is a sharp and dramatic turn to the right.

Encourage your students to use an active voice (*Come!*) to communicate change of direction to the dog.

Week 3: Student Notes

Food is very important for reinforcing new learning. We show the dog a new job and we use food. This gets the dog's attention and the dog learns the job quickly and enthusiastically in order to get the food reward. However, as soon as we *know* that the dog really understands the desired performance, it's time to start cutting back on food rewards to the extent that the dog isn't sure when he'll get a food reward and when he won't. This is called variable or random reinforcement; and, believe it or not, it will actually increase the dog's desire to perform.

Have you ever gone to a drive-through window at a bank or fast food restaurant where they give you a biscuit for the dog? Notice what starts to happen over time. The dog can be sleeping in his crate in the back of the car, but he'll jump up and be attentive at toll booths and every other type of drive-through window you stop at. He may only get a cookie at one out of every ten stops. But it doesn't matter that he is only *occasionally* reinforced—the possibility that he *might* get a cookie is actually a stronger motivator than if he got one every time.

Artist: Jo Ann Mather

Constant reinforcement with a food reward is only necessary while the dog is learning a particular skill. If you continue to give the dog a food treat *every* time he does the job, many dogs will lose some enthusiasm and start just going through the minimal motions necessary to get the reward. The dog is performing the job correctly, but with little enthusiasm. On the other hand, it is critical that you don't completely stop rewarding the dog for performing a job correctly. For example, right now your dog may be extremely reliable at waiting in the contact zones for a release. However, if you decided today to never again give the dog a cookie for waiting in the zone, at some point the dog *will* stop waiting. It might take a week or a few months, but over time that desired behavior you carefully patterned will start to disappear. These are hard lessons for the human trainer.

It's the skill of the trainer to keep track of important statistics about the training. Are you asking the dog to learn something new? Use food. Does your dog understand what you are asking him to do? If in your opinion the answer is "yes", then it's time to give the food reward in an unpredictable pattern.

The dog's complete joy in getting food can be transferred to praise. As you give the dog a treat, you say "Good dog!". Do this consistently and when it comes time to withhold the food, the praise "Good dog!" will communicate to the dog that he did the job right.

The 180° Turn

This week in class you learned to execute a 180° turn in an agility sequence. If you've been doing your backyard exercises from the Student Notes, you may recognize that you have already developed a 180° turn—When you send your dog out to jump and you move out to the side and call your dog back, you have made a 180° turn. The chief difference between this turn and what you did in class, is that in class you asked your dog to perform another obstacle after the turn. But now you're going to do that same thing in your backyard.

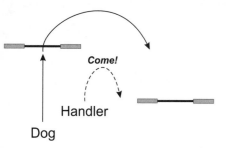

As shown in the illustration on the left, you (the handler) should move towards the first jump with your dog. Then move out to the side and turn around to the next jump, using the *Come!* command to turn the dog to follow you.

Notice that the second jump is slightly recessed so that if the dog turns tightly, he will have a fair approach to the second obstacle.

It's important to recognize that you really want your dog turning to follow you with great enthusiasm and spirit. With this in mind, you should be careful *never* call your dog back to you in order to punish him or to do something that the dog sees as unpleasant (such as getting a bath or having his nails trimmed). Doing so will make your dog reluctant to want to come to you; and even if he does come, he'll do so slowly with a loss of spirit.

If for some reason, you must reprimand your dog, go and get him. Then do the reprimanding.

Weave Poles on the Right

Artist: Jaci Cotton

A lot of folks will claim that their dogs cannot weave while working on their right side. Those of us who have done a lot of formal obedience with our new agility dog will feel challenged when it comes to performing this complex obstacle with the dog on the "off-side".

You should get it in your mind quite early in your training career that your dog *will* be exceptional in performing the weave poles and that your dog *will* weave while on your right side. However, you need to get all the bugs worked out of the performance in the privacy of your backyard.

At first your dog will be quite surprised when you get on the "wrong" side. He may exit the weave poles as though he had no idea what he is supposed to do with them. You have to be patient and understand that this is a huge intellectual leap for the dog. Put a leash back on the dog and begin doing repetitions with your dog working on the off-side. Do this every day and it will only be a short matter of time before your dog is entirely comfortable with doing the weave poles regardless of what side you are working.

Intermediate Agility Workbook

Week 4: Instructor Notes

Just as in your introductory agility classes, in your intermediate classes you still need to be prepared for the ups and downs of learning. What a dog did happily and brilliantly one week, may perplex him the next week.

During these "downs" in the training process, it is important for you to help the handlers be patient with the dogs. The handlers are beginning to get the feel for success and are often very discouraged when their dog has a bad week.

You must be a master of motivation. You are the person on the spot. You are the answer man or woman. If the dog doesn't learn the performance by the numbers, one-two-three, you must be able to specify the remedial path, reassure the handler, and keep the training on track. It is a fact that most novice agility handlers leave the sport because of early disappointments.

Artist: Nancy Krouse-Culley

Usually the answer is the same. Have patience. Don't be in a big hurry. Be prepared to stay on the same training step until the dog *gets it*. Be prepared to back up a training step, or even two. Go slowly. It is important to work on building a strong foundation in spite of the fact that the intermediate student wants to get on with the more impressive stuff.

The students who have seen agility or who are "macho" (this applies to both sexes) about their dog's ability are often the most difficult to slow down. It isn't easy for them to understand how important it is. Explain it and explain it again. Be direct and be subtle.

	Set 1	Set 2	Set 3
Week 4	**Weave Poles and Tunnel** **Reversing Flow** *Obstacles Required:* pipe tunnel, weave poles, A-frame, dogwalk, see-saw, long jump, one winged jump	**Half Circle Sequence** **Blind Cross** 🐾 *Obstacles Required:* pipe tunnel, spread hurdle, one winged jump, tire, collapsed tunnel *Note:* Minor equipment movement is required between exercises.	**Send to Jump** **Speed Circle Variation** **Static Cross** 🐾 *Obstacles Required:* five winged jumps, table *Note:* Major equipment movement is required between exercises.

Organizational Notes

A major theme of the exercises this week is the **cross**, a maneuver in which the handler crosses the path of his dog. Ensure that your instructors are familiar with these concepts before class. Have a pre-practice that allows your instructors to rehearse, if necessary.

Don't forget to review your Progress Worksheets prior to class. There are very likely some dogs that may be having trouble with specific obstacles. Exercises might be too advanced or too simple for your class. You should simplify or add complexity as the individual case warrants. Discuss these issues with all the instructors so that everyone is aware of problem areas.

Start the training session by doing the control exercise on page 53 with *all* students. Then break into groups for the training sets, if you're going to work multiple sets simultaneously.

NOTE: Set 2 will require frequent (but minor) equipment movement between exercises. Set 3 will require major equipment movement between exercises.

Week 4: Progress Worksheet

Instructors: **Date:**

Handler and Dog	Present	Notes

GENERAL NOTES:

Week 4: Facility Layout

One square = 10'

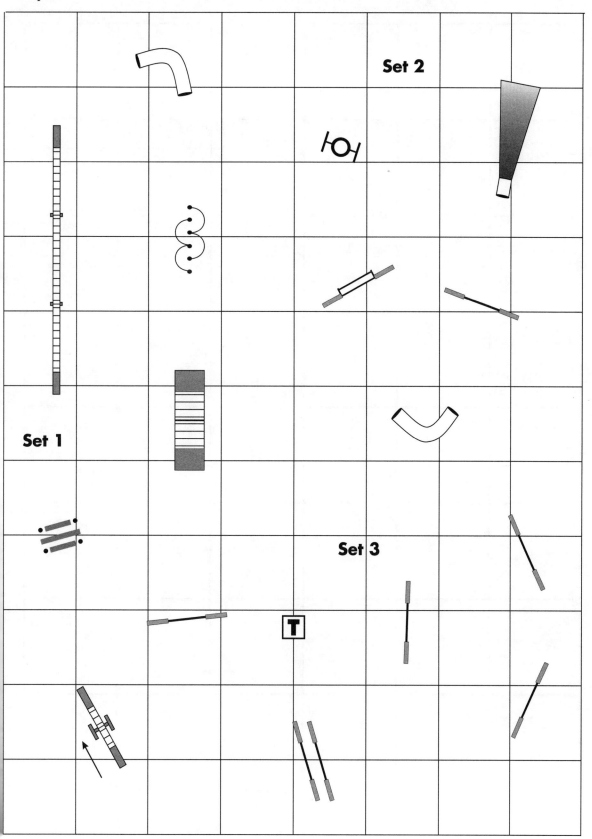

Week 4: Facility Layout Worksheet

Design your Facility Layout using a 1" = 10' scale (standard agility template)

Intermediate Agility Workbook

Week 4: Exercises

Start the class by doing the control exercise with everyone. Then break into smaller groups if you're going to work the training sets simultaneously.

Control Exercise

Start the class with an obedience warm-up exercise. Dogs will work *off-lead*.

- Have your students free heel their dogs into the field of equipment. Don't work in a line—allow them to go where they will. Allow the dogs to sniff and to inspect the equipment, but keep the dogs off the equipment.

- Heel the dogs at attention into a long line. You need 8' to 10' between the dogs.

- *Down!* the dogs. Instruct handlers to leave their dogs and walk about 15', forming a line facing the dogs.

- Staying in a line, have the handlers turn and march around to one end of the line of dogs, and then weave in and out between the dogs. If a dog gets up, that dog's handler should return to the dog, place him back in a down, and then stay with his dog for the rest of the exercise.

- Instruct your students to return to their dogs.

- End of exercise. Praise and release the dogs.

Mark your worksheets for dogs having difficulty with control.

Set 1

Your set consists of two exercises that use the same equipment. No equipment movement will be required except to reverse the direction of the see-saw when the direction of the exercise changes.

Remember that the dog's attention and the handler's control of the dog are important objectives of this set. Because it is a long sequence your students will want to run, go fast, and feel the wind in their hair. This is fine as long as they can maintain control of the dog. You will have to be the judge.

You'll be working with contact obstacles in your set. Remember that your students should reward their dogs only in the contact zone of the descent ramps. The dog is not permitted to leave the contact zone without a quiet release from his handler. If the dog bails off early he should be picked up and placed back on the contact zone.

Weave Poles and Tunnel

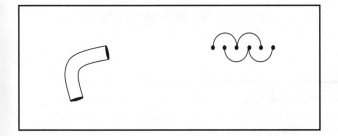

The purpose of this exercise is to review the weave poles. Remind your students that *next week* there will be a competition that features the weave poles. This exercise further introduces the dog to the concept of sequencing *after* weave pole performance.

1. With the dog on his left, each handler does the weave poles. As soon as the dog clears the last pole, the handler praises the dog and then sends him on to the tunnel. The handler should meet the dog as it comes out of the tunnel with praise and a food treat.

2. With the dog on his right, each handler does the weave poles. As soon as the dog clears the last pole, the handler praises the dog and then sends him on to the tunnel. The handler should meet the dog as it comes out of the tunnel with praise and a food treat.

Reversing Flow

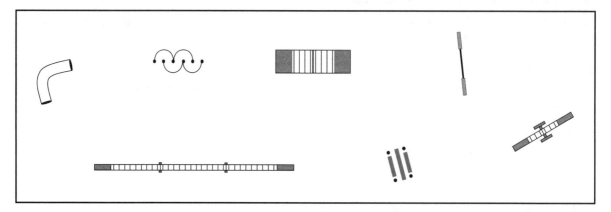

This exercise presents a complex sequencing problem to your students. You will work this circular sequence in both directions. What are the differences between the two flows?

Instruct your students to use variable reinforcement in the course of the sequence. In other words, handlers should sometimes reward the dog with food and sometimes with just praise—except in the case of the contact obstacles, where handlers should still be rewarding the dog in *each* down-side yellow contact zone You should pay attention. Handlers should not be chastising their dogs. There should be plenty of praise.

1. The first sequence starts at the see-saw going towards the long jump. Each handler performs the first three obstacles in the sequence: see-saw–long jump–dogwalk. Your students should require their dogs to wait for a quiet release in the yellow zones of both the contact obstacles.

2. Each handler does the next four obstacles: tunnel–weave poles–A-frame–jump. Again, require that the dog wait for a quiet release in the down contact of the A-frame.

3. Now have each handler put it all together, the see-saw through the bar jump, working the set in a clockwise direction (the dog will be on the handler's left).

   Now turn the see-saw around so you can reverse the direction of the flow.

4. The second sequence starts with the bar jump going towards the A-frame. Each handler performs the first three obstacles: jump–A-frame–weave poles. Require that the dog wait for a quiet release in the down contact of the A-frame.

5. Each handler does the next four obstacles: tunnel–dogwalk–long jump–see-saw. Again, require that the dog wait for a quiet release in the yellow of the contact obstacles.

6. Now have each handler put it all together, the bar jump through the see-saw, working the set in a counter-clockwise direction (the dog will be on the handler's right).

Set 2

Your set consists of two exercises that use largely the same equipment. Some minor equipment movement will be required between exercises. You'll be using the spread hurdle. Please refer to page 110 in the Appendix for a discussion of the height and depth at which the bars need to be set.

Note that the "Blind Cross" exercise is a somewhat advanced. If your students are struggling, simplify the exercise so that it ends on a successful and positive note. The exercise can be redesigned as a simple sequence in which the dog will perform only the first three obstacles. Be sure to mark your worksheet if you have to simplify any exercise. It might be necessary to try the exercise again, at a later date.

You'll be working with contact obstacles in your set. Remember that your students should reward their dogs only in the contact zone of the descent ramps. The dog is not permitted to leave the contact zone without a quiet release from his handler. If the dog bails off early he should be picked up and placed back on the contact zone.

Half-Circle Sequence

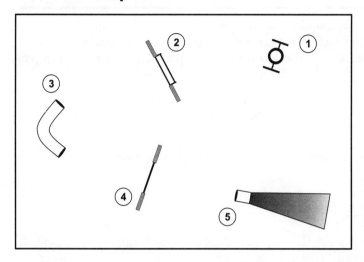

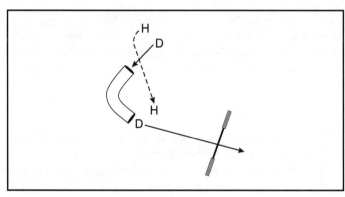

The purpose of this exercise is to work the dog on the off-side (the handler's right) in a short sequence.

Though there are only five obstacles in the sequence, each is different. The exercise will expose any timidness in dogs to perform a particular obstacle.

If you get through several repetitions and it seems too boring, introduce a handling challenge. Put it this way to your students: What if you start the sequence with your dog on your left? You wouldn't really want to run all the way around the pipe tunnel. You'd be moving way too slow, or at least forcing your dog to run a lot slower than you want him to run. Instead, while the dog is in the tunnel, the handler has an opportunity to execute a blind cross.

A **blind cross** is when a handler changes sides to his dog while the dog is in a tunnel and can't see him. To execute this cross, the handler starts the sequence with his dog on the left. As the dog enters the pipe tunnel, the handler steps inside the dog's path. *Voilà!* The dog will now be on the handler's right when it exits the tunnel.

Blind Cross 🐾

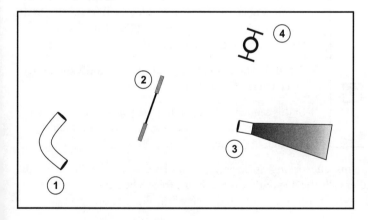

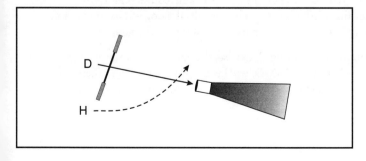

In this exercise, the handler will start with his dog on his left, put the dog into the pipe tunnel, over the jump, and into the collapsed tunnel. Now the fun begins. The sequence calls for a sharp left turn after the collapsed tunnel. It would be very inefficient for the handler to run around the chute of the collapsed tunnel. Not only would he risk a collision with his dog, but the maneuver would take too long.

Before you start, demonstrate a blind cross at the collapsed tunnel—as the dog enters the collapsed tunnel, the handler will cut across the entry of the tunnel and be in position to call the dog through the tire. Advise your students that they should use a little voice to notify their dogs that they've changed sides. Don't be concerned if the dog initially turns right as it exits the tunnel and then runs across the fabric chute to get to the tire jump.

Repeat the exercise three or four times.

Set 3

In this set, you have three exercises that use the same equipment. However, frequent equipment movement will be required during class. Brief your students immediately that they will be moving the equipment between the exercises. You will lay the jump bars on the ground to indicate where to position jumps. Instruct your students to move the jump standards into place.

Note that the "Static Cross" exercise is somewhat advanced. If your students are struggling, simplify the exercise so that it ends on a successful and positive note. The exercise can be redesigned by breaking it down into two separate sequences: two jumps to the table; and then beginning with the table, over the two jumps.

Remember to mark your worksheet if you have to simplify any exercise. It might be necessary to try the exercise again, at a later date.

Send to Jump

Set up a single bar jump and perform the following steps:

1. Allow each handler in the group to put his dog over the jump. As the dog clears the jump, the handler should step out to the left and call his dog back to him. Praise and treat the dog.

2. Now draw a line 5' away from the jump. Have your students send the dog over the jump from behind the line. As the dog clears the jump, the handler should step out to the left and call his dog back to him. Praise and treat the dog. If the dog refuses the jump, the handler should cross the line and put his dog over the jump. It's important for the handler to step out to the side so that the dog does not turn around and perform the jump again when the handler calls him (called a back-jump).

Speed Circle Variation

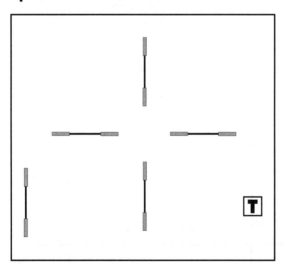

In this exercise, you'll do a variation of the speed circle that is slightly different than what you've done the past three weeks. However, the objectives are essentially the same: control and motivation.

Notice that there are four jumps in the circle, and two obstacles outside the circle: a jump and the table. Called terminal obstacles because the dogs will be starting and ending each sequence at one of these obstacles, these are traps for the dog if the handler isn't careful.

Remind your students to use *Come!* to notify their dogs of a change of direction.

In this sequence, you will require your students to take at least one control break each time they put their dogs through the circle.

1. Start each dog on the table. With the dog on his left working clockwise, the handler does the first three jumps in the circle. After the third jump, the handler calls the dog out for praise and a treat. The handler then finishes the last jump in the circle and exits over the outside jump on the left of the illustration

2. Start each dog at the jump outside the circle. With the dog on his right working counterclockwise, the handler does the first three jumps in the circle. After the third jump, the handler calls the dog out for praise and a treat. The handler then finishes the last jump in the circle and exits by finishing on the table.

3. Start each dog on the table. With the dog on his left working clockwise, the handler does all four jumps in the circle and then finishes on the table. Have the handler briefly *Down!* his dog on the table and then quickly turn and run the set in the other direction—counterclockwise—finishing on the table once again.

Static Cross 🐾

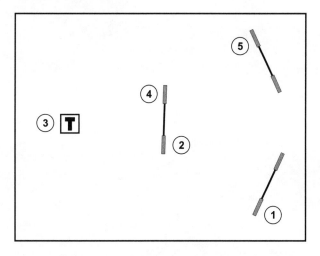

It's time to introduce your students to the concept of crossing the dog's path. A cross is the action of the handler crossing the path of the dog in order to change sides to the dog. In this sequence, the handler will cross the path of the dog while the dog is on the table. This is called a **static cross**. The handler chooses to cross the path of the dog because he doesn't want to walk all the way around the table while the dog is on the table.

This exercise teaches the handler to be somewhat bold; that he can move while his dog is in a *Down!* or *Sit!* on the table. It will increase the handler's confidence and have him taking a solid down-stay and sit-stay very seriously.

For this exercise:

- Do not permit the handler a lead-out.

- Have handlers start with the dog on their left side.

- *Down!* the dogs on the table.

- Have handlers change sides to the dog while the dog is down on the table.

Do several repetitions of the exercise. If time permits, the sequence can be run in reverse order with the dog on the handler's right.

WEEK 4

Week 4: Student Notes

Learning is stressful!

It's been so long since most of us have been in school that we forget what a stressful thing learning can be. In school, we crammed new information into our heads at a rate that boggles the mind. We were tested on what we learned, which made it all the more stressful.

Artist: Nancy Krouse-Culley

It's a good bet that when you were studying for exams you were pensive, pained, and serious. No matter how satisfying and rewarding the information you learned, getting there in the first place had plenty of stress associated with it.

For your dog, learning obedience and agility and other tasks is stressful. It's important for you as the trainer to understand that your dog will go through periods of tension and stress as he learns new exercises. For example, it's not uncommon for dogs to shut down and sometimes run to their crates or cars during training. Other dogs may stop working and choose to sniff the ground or to go visit spectators, all the while ignoring you. Other signs of stress include: the dog's ears plastered to his head; the dog's tail tucked between his legs; the dog salivating, licking his lips, yawning, or panting; and possibly even groveling or a creeping posture.

As part of your training program, you need to develop some kind of regular unstressing activity or pattern of activities that allows the dog to forget about the lesson for awhile and just have fun. Play tug-of-war. Throw a ball or Frisbee™ for your dog. Go for a free-heeling walk in the woods or park—allow the dog to sniff around and investigate things without you jerking constantly at his leash. If you sit to rest awhile, don't just throw him back in the crate; let him sit or lay between your legs as you rest.

On the other hand, don't become overly preoccupied if your dog's tail droops a bit during your training sessions. The dog won't necessarily be upbeat and happy every second. Remember that it's a stressful activity. If you think back on it, it's unlikely that you had a big grin on your face every second you were in school. Don't expect your dog to do so either.

Changing Sides

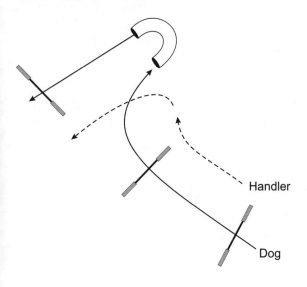

Handler

Dog

This week in class you learned to change sides to your dog. That is, you started a sequence with your dog working on one side of you and then finished the sequence with your dog on the other side. That means your path and the dog's path crossed somewhere in the sequence. The following is an exercise you can do in your own backyard. It does, however, require a pipe tunnel. Hopefully, you've gone out and purchased one of those $20 toy tunnels from Toys 'R Us™.

The dog will be on your left for the first three obstacles. After the tunnel, however, the dog has to turn in a new direction to get to the next obstacle. You could run all the way around the tunnel if you're quick enough. But most of us are considerably slower than our dogs, so we'd just be slowing our dogs down. Instead, put your dog in the tunnel and then just turn and head away towards the final jump. Praise your dog enthusiastically and give him a treat for successfully performing this sequence.

Last Chance Weave Poles Exercise

You should know by now that *next* week in your class, you'll get to participate in a competition that features the weave poles without any channel wires. If you've been doing your homework, then you are already prepared for this challenge. Now, do you want a competitive advantage?

Here are some last minute tuning hints for you.

- Make two lines parallel with the weave poles, 5' away from the poles, on either side. (You can use string, surveyor's tape, duct tape, or even baby powder to mark the lines for yourself.) Now, command your dog to *Weave!*. You can move forward with your dog, but you should stay on the outside of the lines while your dog performs the weave poles. Try this exercise with the dog on the left side and the right side.

  Can your dog really weave? Or, do you need to be right next to the dog to coach him through the poles?

- If you were successful with the previous exercise, now try sending your dog to do the weave poles all by himself. You should remain a few feet away from the entrance of the poles and let the dog go ahead of you. Hopefully, he'll continue down the entire line of poles by himself. If the dog does this for you, you should give him enthusiastic praise and a bonanza food treat.

If your dog can't do these things right now, it's not all that important. These are longer term objectives that you'll want to accomplish in another month or two. If your dog *will* do either of these for you, you should be commended. You've done well with your training program.

A FINAL HINT: It is not necessary for you to crouch down over your dog as he does the weave poles. You should stand up straight and move with your dog. Your frame should face forward towards the end of the poles, rather than sideways towards the dog. It's okay for you to use your voice to encourage your dog through the poles.

Artist: Jaci Cotton

Intermediate Agility Workbook

Week 5: Instructor Notes

As an instructor, you must be a vigilant observer. There are a number of bad handling habits to be watchful for during class. These habits are hard to break and can cost the handler a clean run later in his agility career. It's your job to help handlers recognize and break these habits. Because many handlers aren't consciously aware of many of their actions and movements, at first you'll need to point out the bad habit *while* it's actually happening rather than after the fact. Freeze-frame the action by asking the handler to stop in his tracks so you can show him the problem.

Artist: Jo Ann Mather

While you may get tired of saying the same thing over and over again, some handlers will need to hear it 50 times before it truly sinks in. You'll know you've been successful when the handler makes the mistake, but immediately realizes it and tells you what he did wrong—a self-correction!

- **Hovering**—This is the tendency of a handler to bend over the dog, hang over the dog, and basically get in the dog's space. You see it a lot in weave pole performance where the handler's knee or leg may even make contact with the dog (that's a fault in competition). You'll also see cases where the handler, encroaching the dog's space, pushes the dog off-course to another obstacle. Encourage even handlers with small dogs to stand up straight and keep their body facing in the direction of the course flow—not leaning over and facing the dog.

- **Futzing**—This is when a handler spends five minutes getting the dog in a certain spot and position to start the exercise. You'll often see this same handler take another five minutes as he walks slowly backwards onto the course saying *Stay...Stay...Stay...Stay*. In training, handlers need to practice being very efficient in setting up their dogs. When it's his turn in line, each handler should step up to the start of the exercise, place his dog on a *Wait!* or *Stay!*, and then go. In competition, this type of delay of game can be faulted.

- **Follow-me finger pointing**—This is when a handler feels compelled to keep a finger or hand extended out in front of the dog's face throughout an entire sequence. A quick and definitive hand signal is good, but keeping the arm extended all the time is not necessary or desirable. And, in fact, significant leading—as it's called in competition—can be faulted.

- **Flailing and flopping**—This is when the handler's arms and/or legs are flying and pointing in opposite directions, totally confusing (and sometimes scaring) the dog. This handler will often give hand signals by motioning wildly with the arm furthest away from the dog—you know, the arm the dog can't see! Flailing and flopping is often accompanied by shrieking and screaming (also a bad habit).

	Set 1	Set 2	Set 3
Week 5	**Anticipation**	**Collapsed Turn**	**Working Flows**
	Obstacles Required: two winged jumps, weave poles, table, pipe tunnel	*Obstacles Required:* collapsed tunnel, long jump, one winged jump	*Obstacles Required:* A-frame, spread hurdle, dogwalk see-saw, tire, four winged jumps

Organizational Notes

Start the training session by doing the control exercise on page 65 with *all* students. Next, do the Weave Pole Knockout with all students. You should have a knockout bracket ready to run the competition. Refer to "How to Run a Knockout Competition" on page 66.

After the knockout, break into groups for the training sets, if you're going to work multiple sets simultaneously. Normally each set has two exercises. This week, however, to accommodate the knockout competition there is only one exercise per set.

Week 5: Progress Worksheet

Instructors: **Date:**

Handler and Dog	Present	Notes

GENERAL NOTES:

Week 5: Facility Layout

One square = 10'

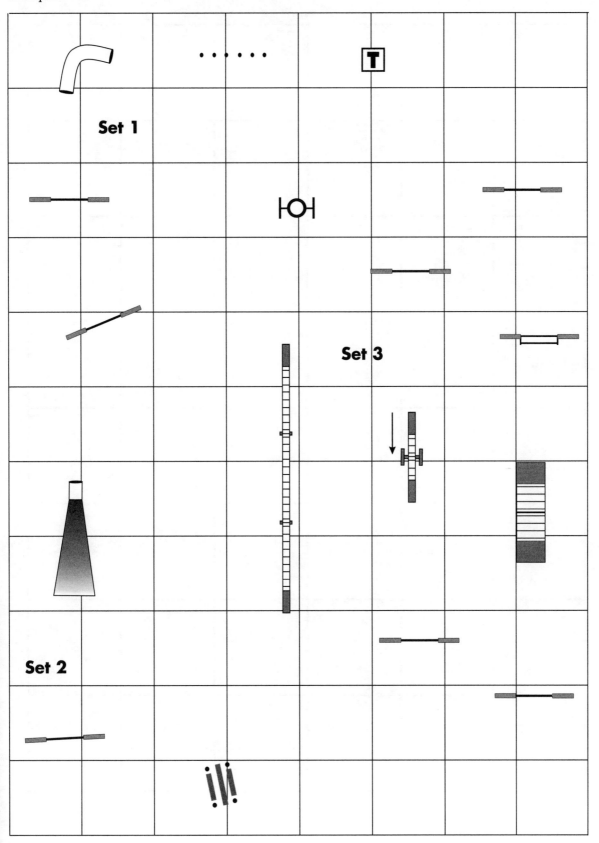

Week 5: Facility Layout Worksheet

Design your Facility Layout using a 1" = 10' scale (standard agility template)

Week 5: Exercises

Start the class by doing the control exercise with everyone. Then run the knockout game. Afterwards, break into smaller groups if you're going to work the training sets simultaneously.

Control Exercise

Start the class with an obedience warm-up exercise. Dogs will work *off-lead*.

- Have your students free heel their dogs into the field of equipment. Don't work in a line—allow them to go where they will. Allow the dogs to sniff and to inspect the equipment, but keep the dogs off the equipment.

- Instruct the handlers to stop wherever they are, *Down!* their dogs, and then leave their dogs.

- Have handlers walk around the field, walking close to the other downed dogs. If any dog breaks its stay, that dog's handler should return to the dog and put it *back* in a down.

- Instruct the handlers to find a spot at least 30' away from their own dogs.

- One at a time, each handler calls his dog. Praise and hold on to the dog until everyone has recalled their dogs.

End of exercise. Mark your worksheets for dogs that are still having a problem with control.

Weave Pole Knockout

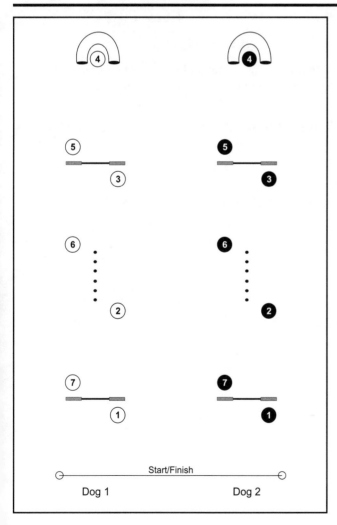

Organize your entire class to run this Weave Pole Knockout. The chief purpose of this exercise is to test everyone's training on the weave poles. You'll immediately know who has and hasn't been practicing at home.

Hopefully, what this competition will accomplish is to embarrass the people who haven't been doing enough training into taking it more seriously. Consequently, it would be counter-productive for you to allow anyone to bow out of the competition.

Set the jumps at 6" for all dogs so that you don't have to worry about changing jump heights. After all, this exercise isn't about jumping; it's about weaving.

The rules are simple. You'll blow a whistle to start the dogs. There will be no faults assessed, but a dog must complete an obstacle correctly before continuing to the next. For example, if a dog drops a jump bar, *the handler* must reset the bar and take the jump again. Likewise, all the weave poles must be completed correctly before the dog moves on.

The first dog to return over the finish line, after having done the course correctly, advances to the next round.

Tell your students that the pipe tunnel can be performed in either direction.

How to Run a Knockout Competition

The way a knockout works is that two dogs run against each other on identical courses. The winning dog advances to the next round. The losing dog sits down, eliminated. That means that half of the competitors advance and half of the competitors are eliminated. You run the competition again and again until there are only two dogs left. Then those two dogs compete to determine the overall winner.

How embarrassing it would be if you got down to the end of the competition and there were *three* dogs and not two. That's the kind of problem *you'll* have if you don't get the numbers right. The key to making the numbers right in a knockout is that the brackets for advancement must be powers of two: 2, 4, 8, 16, 32, 64, 128, and so forth. It's no coincidence that the NCAA basketball championships take a field of 64 teams—64 is one of the magic numbers for a knockout.

You, however, must work with the number of dogs you have available for the competition. If you don't have one of the magic numbers (powers of two), it means that in the *first* bracket some dogs will get an automatic bye. A **bye** means that the dog gets to advance to the next round without having to compete. This might not be entirely fair, but this is the way that it's done.

Here's the formula to determine the number dogs that must compete in the first bracket: $(N–B)*2$.

Let's walk through an example to see how the formula works. Suppose that we have 23 dogs entered in the knockout competition.

1. Find the magic power-of-two number that is equal to or less than the number of competitors. This is the *bracket number* (B in the formula). We'll use 16 because it is the power-of-two number that is equal to or lower than 23.

2. Subtract the bracket number from the *number of competitors* (N in the formula): $23–16 = 7$.

3. Multiply the result of the subtraction by 2. In our example, we get 14.

Set up 14 dogs and handlers to run against one another as shown in the sample knockout scoresheet on the next page. The remaining 9 dogs have a bye in the first round so you automatically advance them to the second bracket as shown in the sample scoresheet.

Making the choice of which dogs get the bye and which have to compete is a problem that you'll have to solve for yourself. You could draw names from a hat or arbitrarily select them. Whatever your selection method, try to be fair as possible.

NOTE: A blank knockout scoresheet for your use is provided on page 68. Because we had to reduce this diagram to fit in the workbook, you may find the scoresheet easier to work with if you take it to a copy shop and have it enlarged onto an 11" x 17" sheet of paper.

Intermediate Agility Workbook

Sample Knockout

FIDO
SABLE
SID
DUFFY
BRANDO
DOODLE
SPLASH
MAX
PETE
SCAM P
DULCIE
HANNY
DICE
NIFTY
LAZER
RUFF
SPIFFY
BOOMER
JESSY
AUGGIE
COCO
FLYER
HANNAH

CHAMPION

WEEK 5

Knockout Scoresheet

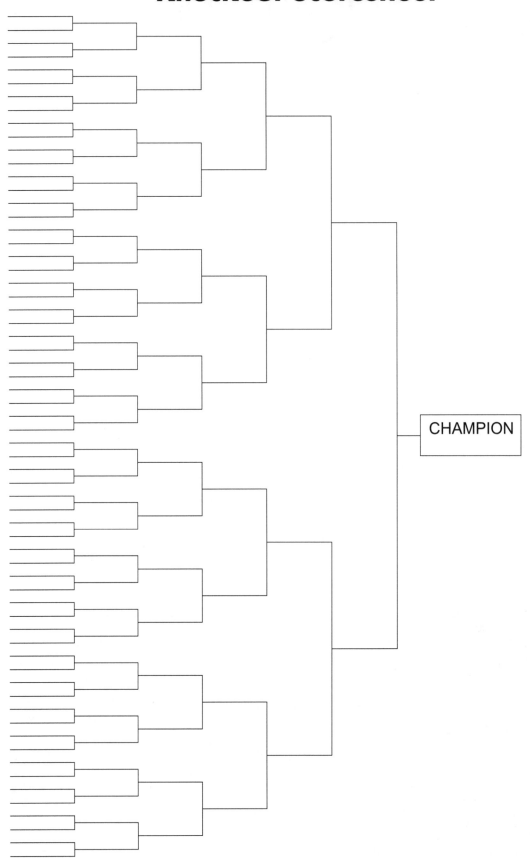

CHAMPION

Intermediate Agility Workbook

Set 1

Your set consists of a single exercise this week.

Anticipation

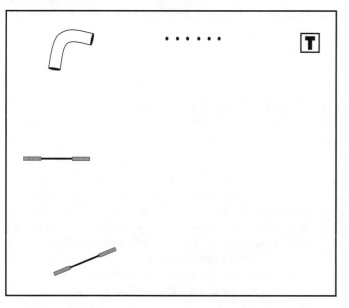

You are going to start this set with a simple review of the pipe tunnel. If necessary, you can pull the tunnel out separately. The purpose of this review is to remind the dog to look to his handler when coming out of the pipe tunnel.

Your students already had a good warm-up with the weave poles. However, anyone who was eliminated from the knockout early on might want to isolate and review the weave poles before starting the exercise.

1. With the dog working on his left, each handler puts his dog through the tunnel. The handler should have a treat and praise ready for the dog when it exits from the tunnel. Repeat this step one or two times.

2. Starting with the jumps and ending on the table, each handler does the entire sequence and then praises and treats the at the end. Repeat this step two or three times. Alternately ask for a *Sit!* or *Down!* on the table.

The opening flow of this sequence will create more speed than the novice handler can cope with to get a clean entry to the weave poles. However, if the dog goes away to the tunnel with any enthusiasm, the handler can step into a good handling position for the weave poles. Remind your students to give the dog an early command for the weave poles and a hand signal that points out the proper entry. Keep in mind that we are working on the communication process between handler and dog. The handler's command must be quick enough to help the dog to make the right choice.

The table, only 8' from the poles, invites the dog to leave the poles early, in anticipation. If the dog breaks out of the weave poles early, the handler should call the dog back and do the weave poles again. This correction should happen without any harshness or emotion.

3. Now, reverse the direction of the sequence so that each handler begins with the dog on the table and ends with the two jumps. Again, the handler gives the dog praise and a treat at the end of the sequence. Repeat this step two or three times.

Now the tunnel will invite the dogs to anticipate and leave the poles early. Again, make a gentle and quiet correction, requiring the dog to do the weave poles before going on.

Set 2

Your set consists of a single exercise.

You'll be working with contact obstacles in your set. Remember that your students should reward their dogs only in the contact zone of the descent ramps. The dog is not permitted to leave the contact zone without a quiet release from his handler. If the dog bails off early he should be picked up and placed back on the contact zone.

Collapsed Turn

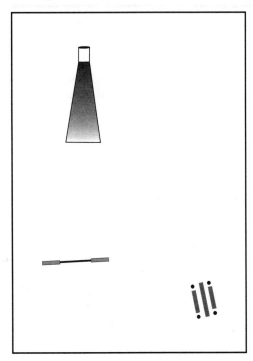

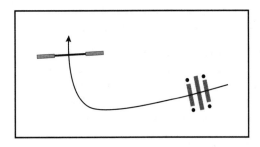

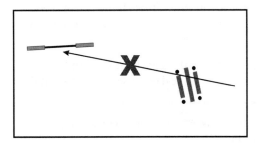

Before starting this exercise, do a quick review of the collapsed tunnel. Then run the first sequence. The purpose of this set is to work on a simple turn in a sequence.

1. With the dog on his right, each handler puts the dog through the tunnel. Handlers should put their dogs through the tunnel with a lot of enthusiasm and they should have a treat and praise ready for the dog when it exits the fabric chute. Repeat one or two times.

2. Starting with the collapsed tunnel and ending with the long jump, each handler does the entire sequence and then gives the dog praise and a treat at the end.

   Remind your students to push forward towards the bar jump after the tunnel and give a good signal to the dog. Often a novice handler will start to turn too early, causing the dog to turn before taking the jump. As soon as the dog is committed to the bar jump, the handler should turn and push towards the long jump. Getting ahead of the dog by a step or two will impel the dog to more speed, which he will need to clear the long jump. The handler should keep moving until the dog is clear of the long jump.

3. Now reverse the direction of the collapsed tunnel so that each handler can run the sequence in the opposite direction: long jump–bar jump–collapsed tunnel.

   Handlers should lead out a bit to give the dog plenty of room to build up speed for the long jump. Talk to your students about putting the dog on a path that initially sends him away from the second jump so that there is plenty of room to square up for the jump as shown in the illustration on the left. Explain the drawbacks of heading the dog at the bar jump in a straight line (increases the possibility of knocking bar, failing to clear the long jump, or having the dog refuse the bar jump because he doesn't have enough room for a good take-off).

   As the dog is out far enough and square to the second jump, the handler should turn, call the dog to *Come!*, and give a command to *Jump!*. Make sure that handlers don't let up at the tunnel. They should give a good hand signal to get the dog into the tunnel.

Set 3

Your set consists of a single exercise. You'll be using the spread hurdle. Please refer to page 110 in the Appendix for a discussion of the height and depth at which the bars need to be set.

Your students should no longer be putting food in the down-side contact zones at this stage of their training. Rather, they should have a food treat ready in hand for the dog. Ensure that your students are not allowing their dogs to leap off the contact obstacle without permission. If the dog bails off early he should be picked up and placed back on the contact zone.

Most of your students should be doing the see-saw with relative confidence. If this is not the case mark your worksheet to indicate who is having trouble. It might be necessary to have a remedial session with problem dogs.

Working Flows

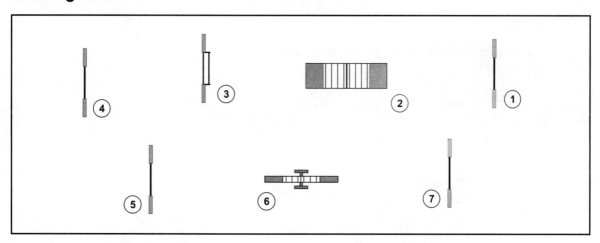

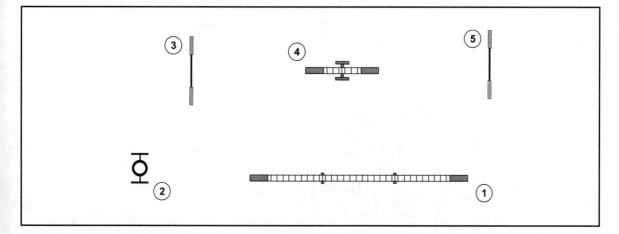

1. Have each handler perform the sequence that starts with the jump and A-frame.

2. Have each handler perform the sequence that starts with the dogwalk.

3. Alternately repeat each sequence until you run out of time with your group.

These are longer sequences than your students are accustomed to running. They will want to run, to feel the wind in their hair. It's your job to bring them back down to earth.

Remind your students to have a treat ready in hand for the dog when it waits in the down-side contact zone of the A-frame, see-saw, and dogwalk.

In both sequences, you should be watching for problems with:

- Timing of commands for each obstacle

- Hand signals

- Allowing the dog to leave the contact zone without a quiet release

Artist: Jaci Cotton

Week 5: Student Notes

When you run, your stride can communicate a lot of information to your dog. As you continue with your agility training, you will discover that many performance problems can result from you changing stride while you are running with your dog.

For example, suppose you have a dog that has trouble clearing the long jump or a spread hurdle. Because you know that your dog has a problem with this obstacle, you may get very nervous as you approach it in a sequence. Without even knowing it, your nervousness causes you to shorten stride. Ironically, your nervousness is seemingly justified as the dog, who also shortens stride, fails to clear the bars. In these instances, it's more important than ever to maintain a strong, consistent stride and push through and past the jump.

Another example is the dog that consistently knocks the last bar of a jump in a sequence. This can be caused by the handler rushing the last obstacle of the sequence. In your anticipation of the end, you speed up and lengthen your stride too much. Likewise, the dog also rushes and lengthens stride, which flattens out his jumping arc and may cause him to knock down a bar.

Artist: Karen Gaydos

These last bar blues can also be caused by the handler slowing down and tiring out before the last obstacle. As you slow down and shorten stride. If the dog is ahead of you, the problem is compounded as the dog will turn around in mid-air and look back for you as he starts losing momentum. Frequently during this turn to look back, a dog will drop his rear feet and knock the bar.

The Shell Game

The hand is quicker than the eye, they say. But is the hand quicker than the nose? There's only one way to find out. Here's a fun game to play at home.

Take three cups. Get your dog's attention as you place the cups upside down on the floor. Next, take your dog's favorite food treat and make a big show out of putting it under one of the cups.

Your dog will be fixed on the cup with the treat with riveted fascination. You're not done yet though. Start to switch the positions of the cups with your two hands, weaving them in and out until any sane person will have lost track of which one of the cups has the treat under it. Then, tell your dog *Find It!*. Your dog should quickly solve the puzzle and knock over the cup with the food tidbit under it, getting a snack for his effort.

If your dog doesn't knock over the correct cup, show him where the food treat was located but don't let him have the treat. Cover it back up and move the cups around again to give him another chance to solve the puzzle.

Your dog will quickly learn the rules of this game. And you will discover that it's pretty hard to fool him. A dog's sense of smell, after all, is about a bazillion times more keen than ours. However, once you get the sense that your dog is trying to solve the puzzle as you move the cups, then it's time to change the rules of the game.

This time put a rubber ball or some other toy under one of the cups. Again, make a big show about putting it under the cup. Again move the cups around until you are positive he can't have kept up with the movement. Tell your dog *Find It!* He's likely to be somewhat more challenged by this version of the game, but he might do a lot better at it than you think he will.

Have fun.

Sequencing With Weave Poles

Up to this point, you've primarily worked on the weave poles in isolation. This exercise makes the weave poles part of a sequence. If your dog has learned the weave poles, this exercise will help him understand that you will frequently ask him to perform the poles in the context of a larger sequence of obstacles.

You will work the exercise shown in the following illustration in both directions.

1. Do the weave poles by themselves. Praise your dog and give him a food treat.

   The jump should not be performed in this first step, though your dog should be able to see clearly that it's there. Remember that one of your objectives is to teach your dog to watch for *your* signal rather than automatically doing the next obstacle in a sequence.

2. Do the weave poles. Praise your dog briefly and then send him over the jump. Step out to the side and call your dog back to you around the jump. Don't let the dog back-jump. Praise your dog warmly and give him a food treat.

3. Now reverse the direction of the exercise. Do the jump by itself. Praise your dog and give him a food treat.

   The weave poles should not be performed in this step.

4. Do the jump, praise your dog briefly, and then send him to do the weave poles. When he's gone down the line of poles praise your dog warmly and give a food treat.

The exercise below builds on the previous one. Don't do this new exercise until you've practiced the first exercise for two or three days. Make sure that you work both exercises with the dog on your right as well as your left.

1. Do the first jump by itself. Praise your dog and give him a food treat.

   The weave poles should not be performed in this step.

2. Do the jump, praise your dog briefly, and then send him to do the weave poles. When he's gone down the line of poles praise your dog warmly and give a food treat. The final jump should not be performed in this step, though your dog should be able to see clearly that it's there.

3. Do the jump, praise your dog briefly, and then send him to do the weave poles. Praise him briefly and send him on to the final jump. Step out to the side and call your dog back to you. Praise your dog warmly and give a food treat. Again, make sure that you don't allow the dog to turn around and come back over the last jump.

Week 6: Instructor Notes

It is usually not a good idea to run courses in training except for reasonably advanced students and for students who are tuning for competition. The intermediate dog has had only two or three months of exposure to agility. While the dog may have mastered all the individual obstacles, putting them all together is an entirely different skill. The intermediate dog is not yet ready for sequences of fourteen to twenty obstacles.

What you actually accomplish when you run courses with dogs that are not ready for it, is to make the dogs fail and to frustrate the handlers. It's conceivable that a handler will give up the sport because the failure is so absolute.

In the introductory program, we introduced dogs to the obstacles and in some instances got the dogs to do short sequences of two and three obstacles. In the intermediate program, dogs are doing sequences of four, five, six, and seven obstacles. So what you are doing in a thoughtful long-range program is slowly increasing the number of obstacles included in a training sequence. The dog gradually becomes accustomed to the fact that his handler will ask him to perform one obstacle after another in longer and longer sequences.

Artist: Valerie Pietraszewska

There will be time enough in the advanced program to do sequences of ten and twelve obstacles. But even in an advanced training program, you should run courses only rarely. Doing smaller sets allows you to isolate problem areas, attend to minor performance issues, and build fundamental skills. If you are doing a course of eighteen or twenty obstacles, you are exposing every conceivable performance problem the dogs are having without being able to be very focused on fixing those problems.

When your students ask you why you don't run courses in practice, you tell them the truth. Tell them, "You're not ready yet."

	Set 1	Set 2	Set 3
Week 6	**Little Feets** **Tunnel Side-Track** 🐾 *Obstacles Required:* tire, spread hurdle, two winged jumps, pipe tunnel *Note:* Minor equipment movement is required between exercises.	**Fast Flow to Weaves** **Dogwalk Sequence** *Obstacles Required:* weave poles, two winged jumps, long jump, dogwalk *Note:* Minor equipment movement is required between exercises.	**Send to Table** **Off-Side Conditioning** **Horseshoe** *Obstacles Required:* table, collapsed tunnel, A-frame, five winged jumps *Note:* Minor equipment movement is required between exercises.

Organizational Notes

This week take a moment to remind your instructors to tell the students how well they are doing. A little bit of praise goes a long way to encourage a student who might feel like he is struggling. It works for dogs, and it works for humans.

Start the training session by doing the control exercise on page 79 with *all* students. Then break into groups for the training sets, if you're going to work multiple sets simultaneously.

Note that all three of the sets will require minor equipment movement between exercises.

Week 6: Progress Worksheet

Instructors: **Date:**

Handler and Dog	Present	Notes

GENERAL NOTES:

Intermediate Agility Workbook

Week 6: Facility Layout

One square = 10'

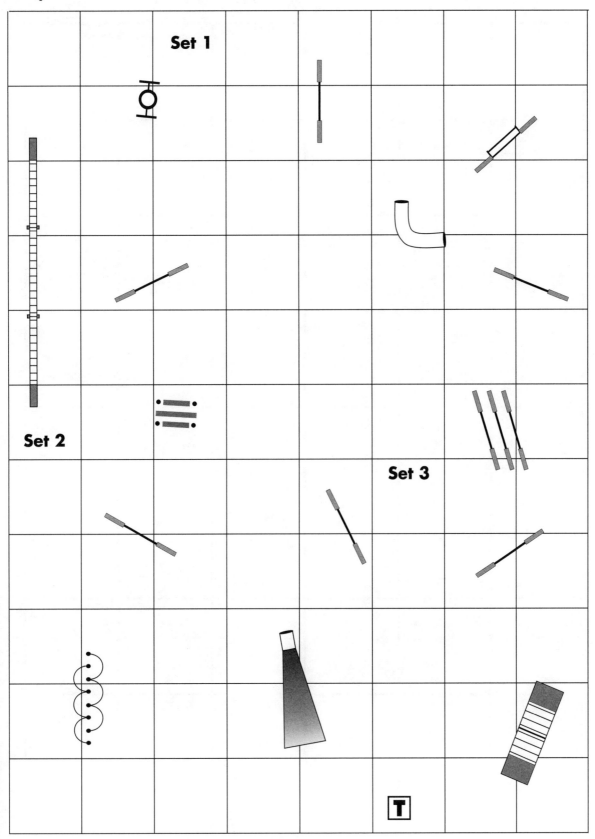

Set 1

Set 2

Set 3

T

Week 6: Facility Layout Worksheet

Design your Facility Layout using a 1" = 10' scale (standard agility template)

Intermediate Agility Workbook

Week 6: Exercises

Start the class by doing the control exercise with everyone. Then break into smaller groups if you're going to work the training sets simultaneously.

Control Exercise

Start the class with an obedience warm-up exercise. Dogs will work *off-lead*.

- Have your students free heel their dogs into the field of equipment. Don't work in a line—allow them to go where they will. Allow the dogs to sniff and to inspect the equipment, but keep the dogs off the equipment.

- Heel the dogs at attention into a long line. You need 8' to 10' between the dogs.

- *Down!* the dogs. Instruct handlers to leave their dogs and walk about 40', forming a line facing the dogs.

- Wait two minutes (the instructor should keep time). If any dog breaks its stay during this time, the handler will collect the dog and hold on to it for the remainder of the exercise.

- Recall the dogs *one* at a time. Each handler commands his dog to *Come!* With any luck, the right dog will get up and come directly to the handler. If the dog does not do so, the handler will go and collect his dog. If the wrong dog comes, that dog's handler will collect his dog and put him back in a down with the other dogs.

Mark your worksheets for dogs having difficulty with control.

Set 1

Your set consists of two exercises that use largely the same equipment. Some equipment movement is required between exercises, but that movement is relatively minor. You'll be using the spread hurdle. Please refer to page 110 in the Appendix for a discussion of the height and depth at which the bars need to be set.

Balance your time with each group so that your students get approximately the same amount of work on each of the exercises.

The "Tunnel Side-Track" exercise is somewhat advanced. If your students are struggling with the exercise, you should simplify the exercise so that it ends on a positive note. The exercise can be redesigned into a simple looping sequence.

Little Feets

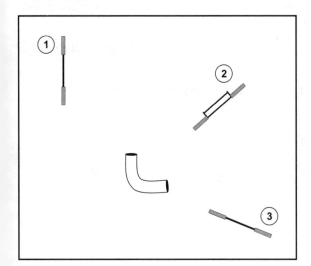

The purpose of this exercise is to gauge each dog's reaction to his handler's movement. It is important that handlers do the exercise as instructed.

Each dog and handler will do *all* of the following steps *before* the next dog and handler in line work the exercise:

1. The handler performs jumps #1 and #2 with the dog on his left. The handler should abruptly turn around (180° with his back to the dog) at jump #2, call the dog out of the sequence, and return to the start of the exercise.

   Be careful not to allow or encourage the dog to back-jump the obstacles in the sequence. You should take note of what happens to the dog's stride as the handler shortens his own stride.

2. The handler performs jumps #1, #2, and #3 with the dog on his left. The handler should abruptly turn around (180° with his back to the dog) at jump #3, call the dog out of the sequence, and return to the start of the exercise.

   Be careful not to allow or encourage the dog to back-jump the obstacles in the sequence. Again, take note of what happens to the dog's stride as the handler shortens his own stride. What did the dog do?

3. The handler performs jumps #1 and #2 with the dog on his left. The handler should abruptly turn right at jump #2, *walk* to the entrance of the tunnel, call the dog, and then put the dog through the tunnel.

4. The handler performs jumps #1, #2, and #3 with the dog on his left. The handler should abruptly turn right at jump #3, *walk* to the entrance of the tunnel, call the dog, and then put the dog through the tunnel.

You should be able to observe a couple of points during this multi-part exercise. The handler's abrupt turn should have some impact on the dog. As the handler anticipates the turn, his stride will shorten. The dog's stride should also shorten.

It's very difficult for many handlers to turn a back to their dogs. But that's exactly what the exercise calls for. You, the instructor, should be the referee of a clean turn.

Tunnel Side-Track 🐾

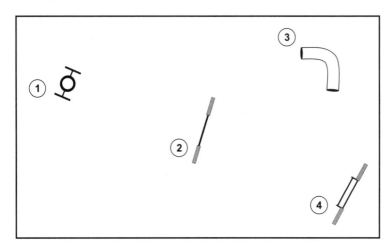

We've tried to establish throughout this intermediate training program that the dog's attention to the handler is pre-requisite to the dog performing the next obstacle in sequence.

Each dog and handler will do *all* of the following steps *before* the next dog and handler in line work:

1. The handler puts the dog through the tire, calls the dog to *Come!* out of the sequence, and then praises and treats the dog.

2. The handler sends the dog over the bar jump, calls the dog to *Come!* out of the sequence, and then praises and treats the dog.

3. The handler puts the dog in the indicated entry to the tunnel, calls the dog to *Come!* out of the sequence, and then praises and treats the dog.

4. The handler sends the dog over the spread hurdle, calls the dog to *Come!* out of the sequence, and then praises and treats the dog.

   After all the dogs in your group have done steps 1–4, change the exercise. Each dog and handler will now do steps 5–8 *before* the next dog and handler in line work the exercise.

5. The handler puts the dog through the tire, calls the dog to *Come!* out of the sequence, and then praises and treats the dog.

6. The handler performs the tire and the bar jump, calls the dog to *Come!* out of the sequence, and then praises and treats the dog.

7. The handler performs the tire, bar jump and tunnel, calls the dog to *Come!* out of the sequence, and then praises and treats the dog.

8. The handler performs the entire sequence: tire–bar jump–tunnel–spread hurdle. At the end, the handler calls the dog to *Come!* and then praises and treats the dog.

Set 2

Your set consists of two exercises that use largely the same equipment. Some equipment movement is required between exercises, but that movement is relatively minor.

Balance your time with each group so that your students get approximately the same amount of work on each of the exercises.

You'll be working with a contact obstacle in your set. Remember that your students should reward their dogs only in the contact zone of the descent ramps. The dog is not permitted to leave the contact zone without a quiet release from his handler. If the dog bails off early he should be picked up and placed back on the contact zone.

Fast Flow to Weaves

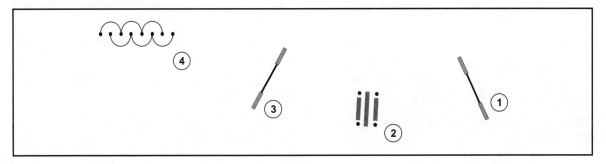

In this exercise, the handler will work on gradually establishing a larger and larger lead-out. The exercise is a fair test of the work the handler has done (at home) working on a good stay for the dog.

If during any step the dog runs around one or more jumps, the handler should very calmly take the dog back and perform the appropriate obstacle(s).

Each dog and handler will do *all* of the following steps *before* the next dog and handler in line work:

1. The handler leads out past the first jump and calls the dog over the jump. The handler then calls the dog to *Come!* out of the sequence and praises and treats the dog.

2. The handler leads out past the long jump and calls the dog over both the bar jump and the long jump. The handler then calls the dog to *Come!* out of the sequence and praises and treats the dog.

3. The handler leads out past the third jump in the sequence and calls the dog over all three jumps. The handler then calls the dog to *Come!* out of the sequence and praises and treats the dog.

4. The handler leads out past the third hurdle in the sequence and stands next to the weave poles. The handler should call the dog over all three hurdles, put the dog through the weave poles, call the dog to *Come!*, and then praise and treat the dog.

   After all the dogs in your group have done steps 1–4, change the exercise. Each dog and handler will now do steps 5–8 *before* the next dog and handler in line work the exercise.

5. The handler leads out past the first jump. The handler should call the dog over the jump and then finish the entire sequence, praising and treating the dog at the end.

6. The handler leads out past the long jump. The handler should call the dog over the two jumps and then finish the entire sequence, praising and treating the dog at the end.

7. The handler leads out past the third jump. The handler should call the dog over all three jumps and then finish the sequence, praising and treating the dog at the end.

8. The handler leads out past the third hurdle in the sequence and stands next to the weave poles. The handler should then call the dog over all three hurdles and put the dog through the weave poles, praising and treating the dog at the end.

Dogwalk Sequence

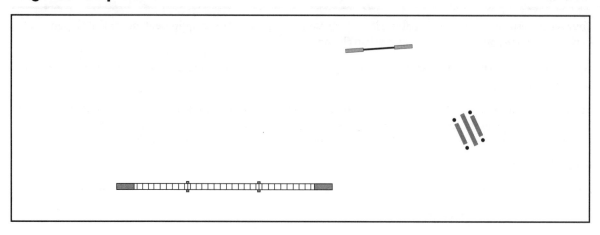

This is a simple sequence that will begin with the dogwalk. After the dogwalk, the dog will either be turned slightly left to the long jump or be turned harder left to the bar jump. The dog should be worked on the handler's right, so that the handler is in best position to direct the dog to the correct jump.

You can explain to your students that this simple maneuver is the culmination of a couple of skills that you have been practicing: 1) the dog should never leave a contact obstacle without a quiet release from his handler; and 2) the dog should direct his attention to the handler after performance of an obstacle, rather than focusing on the next apparent obstacle in sequence.

Remind the handlers to have a treat ready in hand for when the dog pauses in the contact zone. Each handler should perform the following steps:

1. With the dog on his right, each handler puts the dog over the dogwalk. The dog should not leave the contact zone without the quiet release of the handler. The handler should then turn the dog gently left and push over the long jump. Instead of just lunging towards the next obstacle, the handler must get the dog's attention before presenting the long jump to the dog.

2. With the dog on his right, each handler puts the dog over the dogwalk. The dog should not leave the contact zone without the quiet release of the handler. The handler should then turn the dog hard left and push over the bar jump. Instead of just lunging towards the next obstacle, the handler must get the dog's attention before presenting the bar jump to the dog. In this step, it will be especially important to get the dog's attention, since the dog previously performed the long jump and he is going to see the long jump before he sees the bar jump.

3. Repeat steps 1 and 2 several times.

Set 3

Your set consists of three exercises that use largely the same equipment. Some equipment movement is required between exercises, but that movement is relatively minor.

Balance your time with each group so that your students get approximately the same amount of work on each of the exercises.

You'll be working with a contact obstacle in your set. Remember that your students should reward their dogs only in the contact zone of the descent ramps. The dog is not permitted to leave the contact zone without a quiet release from his handler. If the dog bails off early he should be picked up and placed back on the contact zone.

Send to Table

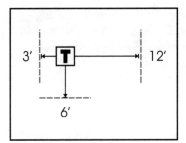

The purpose of this quick exercise is to encourage the dog to go away from the handler to get on the table. This is presented to your students in the nature of a game. Don't require the dogs to *Sit!* or *Down!* on the table.

Before you start, collect a handful of treats from each student. Your job is to be the baitmaster. You'll stand at the table and load it up with goodies that will inspire the dogs to want to be on the table. Make sure that you're ready to snatch the treat away if a dog refuses to get up on the table and tries to grab the treat from the side.

Draw lines on three sides of the table as shown in the illustration: one line should be 3' from the table; a second line should be 6' from the table; and the third line should be drawn 12' from the table.

1. Put all your students in a line at the 6' line. The objective is to send the dog to the table from this line. Everybody will have three chances, one after another, before the next dog goes.

2. If the dog goes to the table, the handler moves to the 12' line for his next try. If the dog does not go to the table, the handler moves to the 3' line for the next try.

3. If the dog goes to the table from the 12' line, for his last turn the handler should send the dog from the 12' line again. If the handler moved to the the 3' line in step 2 and was successful from that point, he should go to the 6' line for his last try.

Off-Side Conditioning and a Sudden Stop

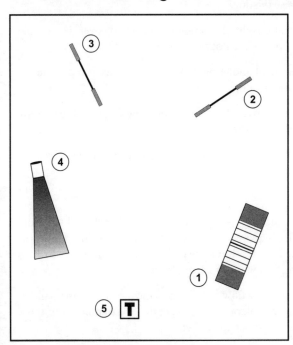

The loopy nature of this sequence will build a lot of speed to the table. Consequently, we should first do some work to get the attention of our dogs.

The sequence demands that the dog be worked on the handler's right. However, start your students on this set without pointing out this fact. Poke liberal fun at anyone who handles their dog on the obedience side. Obviously, that makes the handler run the long way around and makes the dog go slower than is necessary.

A circle implies a constant change of direction. A dog will tend to go in the direction that his nose is pointed. So get your students to work with a command like *Here!* or *Come!* to keep the dogs turning.

Okay, what do you do about the table? The handler, on the inside of the loop, has a tremendous advantage on the dog, who must travel further. There is a good possibility the handler will beat the dog to the table, thus creating a race that might cause the dog to skip on and off the table.

Tell your students for whom speed is a problem to slow down on a fast approach to the table. All they have to do is slow down and let the dog win the race.

Start the dogs at the A-frame. Remind the handlers to have a treat ready in hand for when the dog pauses in the down-side contact of the A-frame.

Students should *Down!* their dogs on the table. Before the handler releases the dog, give each dog a five second count to get them accustomed to this practice.

Horseshoe

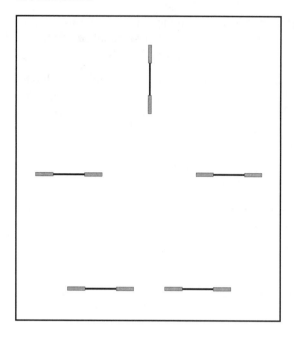

The purpose of this exercise is to command the dog's attention to his handler. Tell your students that they will be using the *Come!* command to make the dog pause in the performance of the obstacles. When a handler says *Come!*, the dog should come directly to the handler and await the next command. If the handler does not give a command, the dog should wait patiently.

The handler will work in the center of this horseshoe configuration.

Each dog and handler will do *all* of the following steps *before* the next dog and handler in line work:

1. Working in a clockwise direction with the dog on his left, the handler puts the dog over one jump. The handler should stop then, tell the dog to *Come!*, and praise the dog.

2. Working in a counterclockwise direction with the dog on his right, the handler puts the dog over two jumps. The handler should then stop, tell the dog to *Come!*, and praise the dog.

3. Working in a clockwise direction with the dog on his left, the handler puts the dog over three jumps. The handler should stop then, tell the dog to *Come!*, and praise the dog.

4. Working in a counterclockwise direction with the dog on his right, the handler puts the dog over four jumps. The handler should stop then, tell the dog to *Come!*, and praise the dog.

5. Working in a clockwise direction with the dog on his left, the handler puts the dog over five jumps. The handler should stop then, tell the dog to *Come!*, and praise and treat the dog.

6. Repeat steps 1–5 with the next dog in line.

If the dog goes on to the next jump without coming to the handler as commanded, the handler should withhold the praise. You should be watching to ensure that the handler is giving an early command for the dog. Timing is very important. The faster the dog is moving, the earlier the handler should be giving a command either to *Jump!* or to *Come!*. The dog should not be expected to change direction without adequate warning.

The handler's posture assists in the delivery of the command. If the flow continues to the next jump, the handler should be pushing forward in the direction of the flow. If the handler is trying to get the dog to pull out of the sequence and come to him, the handler should be standing still or backpedaling.

NOTE: If you have time after completing the exercise, this is a good set for a game of Follow the Leader. The first handler runs a pattern of his choice. One by one, each handler runs the same pattern until a dog faults (knocked bar, off-course, refusal, and so on). The next handler in line then makes a new pattern for the class to follow.

WEEK 6

Week 6: Student Notes

Dog agility is changing the way we think about our dogs. Not only is it helping dog owners all over the world take more responsibility for their dogs, it is opening their eyes to a host of possibilities for giving their dogs work and recreation.

Usually, when you mention the words "dog show" to someone, what immediately comes to mind is one of the conformation events like Westminster. However, conformation shows like Westminster are only one of dozens of types of dog shows. And the difference between conformation and agility is like the difference between participating in a beauty pageant and playing in a game of rugby.

Agility is defined as a performance event in the dog show circuit. Dog owners may train and compete with their dogs in a variety of performance events—scent hurdles, herding, tracking, lure coursing, field trials, and flyball to name only a few.

Agility, however, has a special quality that helps make dog trainers out of dog owners. It attracts people to the sport because it is fast and fun and sporting. It is also "do-able". Through agility

Artist: Jo Ann Mather

training, you learn how to develop that special relationship with your dog that taps into the dog's desire to learn. You also become aware of your role and responsibilities in that relationship.

Ultimately, dog agility will lead you to seek new challenges and to fully explore the potential of your dog. You may seek out other performance events or even aspire to train dogs for rescue work, for police work, for protection, or for guiding the blind or deaf. The possibilities are almost limitless.

Flow Control

A continuing theme at classes has been controlling your dog in a sequence. The reason for this is to teach the dog to listen to you to get permission to do an obstacle, rather than automatically assuming that he is supposed to do the next obstacle in sequence. This is something that you can set up and practice quite easily at home. In the following examples, we are using three bar jumps. However, you can use any three obstacles in a straight line that sets up a flow that would invite the dog to continue on.

Put your dog over the first jump in the sequence and call the dog out to one side. You should practice this working both sides. Use liberal praise and your dog's favorite food treat when he is learning this exercise.

Repeat this step several times.

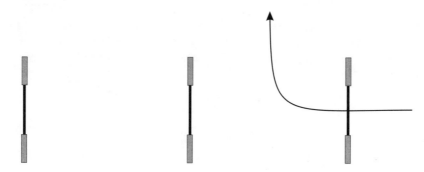

When you can reliably call your dog out of the sequence after the first jump, begin sending your dog over the first two jumps. Again, practice working both sides. Occasionally go back to doing only the first jump to keep your dog guessing and checking with you for permission to take the next jump in the sequence. Use liberal praise and your dog's favorite food treat while learning this exercise.

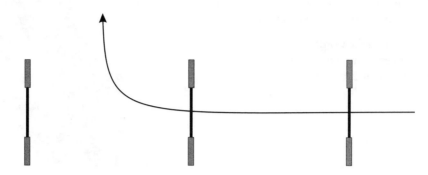

Only when you can reliably call your dog out of the sequence after either the first or second jumps, begin sending him over all three jumps. Practice working both sides. Occasionally go back to doing only the first jump, or only the first two jumps, to keep your dog guessing and checking with you for permission to take the next jump in the sequence. Use liberal praise and your dog's favorite food treat while learning the exercise.

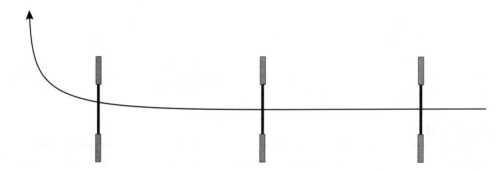

SAFETY NOTE: Your stamina in this exercise is likely to be somewhat greater than your dog's. Your dog is doing all the work, after all. You should spend no more than ten or fifteen minutes each day working on jumping sets like this one. Break it up into two separate daily workouts to give your dog a rest and keep it interesting for him.

Intermediate Agility Workbook

Week 7: Instructor Notes

How important is voice in dog agility? An upbeat voice can motivate a reluctant dog, or throw a tightly wound dog into a frenzy. We rely on voice to give clear and sharp commands, and to signal to the dog where we are on the field. Voice also signals the handler's emotional state to his dog.

Artist: Valerie Pietraszewska

One of your many jobs is to use your powers of observation to *hear* what your students are doing as they talk to their dogs. Here are some things to watch for:

- The handler keeps up a constant string of talk. This blathering doesn't do much to direct the dog. Remind these handlers to cut down the number of words they use. Commands for obstacles and changes of direction are all that are really required, though occasional praise of the dog doesn't hurt at all.

- It's not necessary to say the dog's name before every obstacle. The dog knows that his handler is talking to him. Besides the fact that there's not enough time to get out that many words, it's a good idea to save the dog's name for when the handler *really* needs the dog's attention.

- A dog will react much better to a high-pitched and enthusiastic voice (not the same thing as a shrill or shrieking voice) than to a monotonous voice. This is tough for men because it makes them sound silly and you know that they don't want to look silly in front of a bunch of women and their dogs.

- A loud voice and a low-pitched voice sound threatening to a dog and may make the dog fearful. Even if the handler didn't intend to sound harsh, it should be called to his attention if he does.

- Your students should not use commands that the dog doesn't yet know; for example, a handler saying *Easy...Easy...Easy...Easy* as his dog goes over the dogwalk. Does the dog know what *Easy!* means? Challenge the handler to show you on the flat, with the dog *off-lead*.

Almost every training set should include an instruction to your students to give a clear command for performance of each obstacle. A clear command is a command that is loud enough to hear and that is delivered in a timely fashion. It should be accompanied by other tangible elements of the handler's language, such as a hand signal and a body frame facing in the direction of the flow.

	Set 1	Set 2	Set 3
Week 7	**Turning Game** **A Change of Sides** 🐾 *Obstacles Required:* Four winged jumps, spread hurdle, collapsed tunnel, tire	**Working the Outside** **To Boldly Go** *Obstacles Required:* Dogwalk, table, A-frame, two winged jumps, weave poles	**The Wave** **Turn Backs** *Obstacles Required:* See-saw, pipe tunnel, three winged jumps *Note:* Minor equipment movement is required between exercises.

Organizational Notes

It's time to decide who will move up to a more advanced program and who will repeat the intermediate program. Consult with all your instructors. You should discuss their observations after today's class.

Start the training session by doing the control exercise on page 91 with *all* students. Then break into groups for the training sets, if you're going to work multiple sets simultaneously.

Note that Set 3 will require minor equipment movement between exercises.

Week 7: Progress Worksheet

Instructors: **Date:**

Handler and Dog	Present	Notes

GENERAL NOTES:

Week 7: Facility Layout

One square = 10'

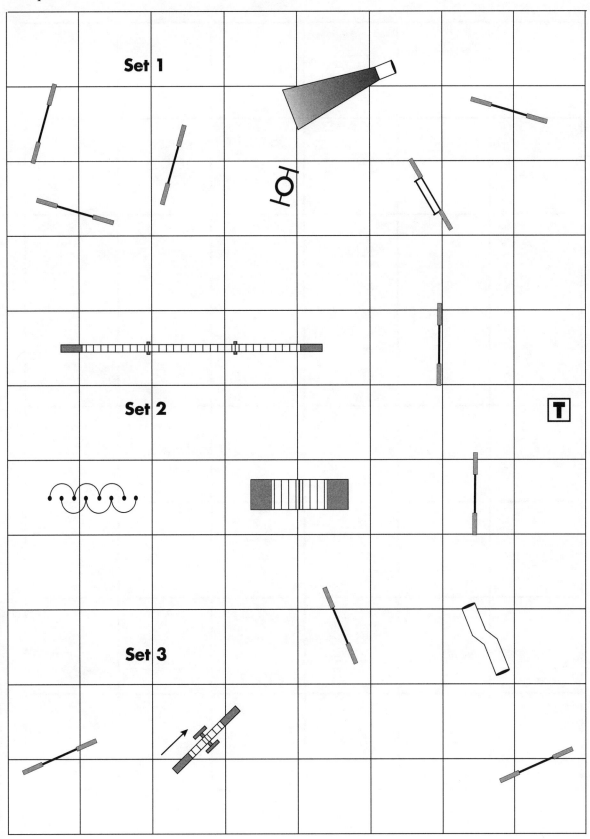

Set 1

Set 2

T

Set 3

Week 7: Facility Layout Worksheet

Design your Facility Layout using a 1" = 10' scale (standard agility template)

Week 7: Exercises

Start the class by doing the control exercise with everyone. Then break into smaller groups if you're going to work the training sets simultaneously.

Control Exercise

Start this class with an obedience warm-up exercise. Dogs will work on leash. This is a simple citizenship test. Handlers should take care that their dogs don't lunge at other dogs or handlers.

• Heel the dogs on-leash into the field away from the equipment.

• Form two lines of the same number of dogs and handlers, facing one another. You need about 20' between the two lines.

• One handler from each line will heel their dogs and meet in the middle. Come to a halt with the handlers facing one another.

• The handlers are to shake hands and then heel their dogs past each other to take a place in the opposite line of handlers and dogs.

End of exercise.

Set 1

Your set consists of two exercises that use the same equipment. No equipment movement is required. You'll be using the spread hurdle. Please refer to page 110 in the Appendix for a discussion of the height and depth at which the bars need to be set.

The exercise called "A Change of Sides" is somewhat advanced. If your students struggle with the exercise, you should simplify it so that you can end on a positive note.

Don't forget that you should be making note of those dogs that should be moving on to a more advanced class, and those dogs that should repeat this intermediate program.

You'll be working with a contact obstacle in your set. Remember that your students should reward their dogs only in the contact zone of the descent ramps. The dog is not permitted to leave the contact zone without a quiet release from his handler. If the dog bails off early he should be picked up and placed back on the contact zone.

Turning Game

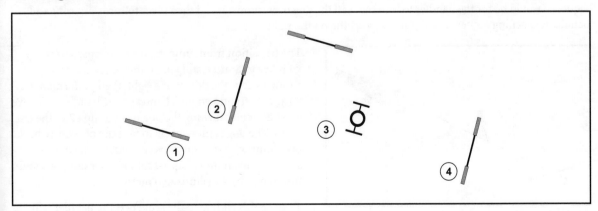

The most powerful command in agility is *Come!*. It's the change of direction command. It's like one of those Newton Laws—to paraphrase it—*A dog in motion in one direction is liable to remain moving in that direction until an outside force acts to move the dog in another direction.*

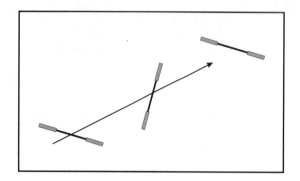

Change of direction is a subtle thing. We have to train our eyes to see it. In this sequence we see a very straight line from #2 to #4. But, in fact, there is also a straight line from #1 to #2 that goes straight on through the dummy jump as shown in the diagram on the left. Point out these lines in the sequence to your students.

Run the sequence several times. Require the handler to start with his dog and to work his dog on the left.

The handler needs to give the dog a strong *Come!* after jump #1. Advise your students to *keep* the dog turning. Another strong *Come!* after jump #2 would be advisable. The timing of this second *Come!* is very important. The handler must communicate the change of direction to the dog *before* the dog has mentally committed to the off-course jump.

A Change of Sides 🐾

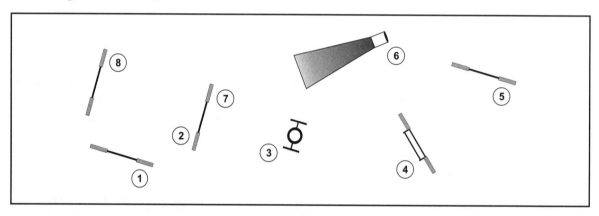

This exercise is a bit more complex than what your intermediate students are used to. Allow your students to walk the sequence and think through how they are going to handle their dogs. Stop and discuss the exercise and handling options with your students.

The turn from jump #1 to jump #2 is easy enough to execute. However, if the handler works the dog on his left, it will put the handler on the long path around jumps #4 and #5. Possibly the best handling strategy for this sequence would be for the handler to lead out, call the dog over jump #1, and then pivot towards jump #2 and handle the opening sequence with the dog working on the right.

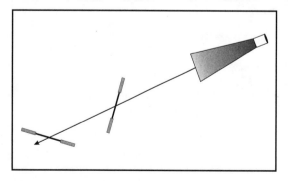

The transition from jump #5 to the collapsed tunnel at #6 is key to a successful end to this sequence. If the handler keeps the dog on his right, then performance of #6 and #7 should go fine. However, the handler will have great difficulty turning the dog from jump #7 to the last jump. The dog is more likely to take the off-course back over jump #1. Point out to your students the line-of-sight trap from the collapsed tunnel, over jump #7, and through jump #1 (illustrated on the left).

To solve this ending to the sequence, the handler will have to change sides to his dog. That is, in the middle of the sequence, the handler will switch the side on which he is working his dog.

WEEK 7

Before you run the exercise, you will demonstrate two possibilities for a change of sides during this exercise. Your students will practice each, and get a feeling for what is most effective for them.

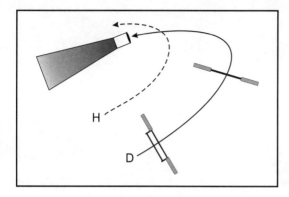

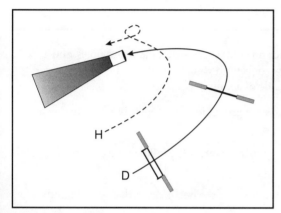

1. Demonstrate for your students a blind cross. That is, after committing the dog into the collapsed tunnel, the handler will step up to the right of the tunnel, effectively putting the dog on his opposite side.

2. Have each handler do one or two repetitions of obstacles #4, #5, and #6 only, practicing the blind cross as illustrated on the left.

3. Now demonstrate for your students a front cross. That is, send the dog over jump #5. As soon as the dog is committed to the jump, the handler will step past the opening of the collapsed tunnel, rotate back clockwise, and call the dog back.

4. Have each handler do one or two repetitions of obstacles #4 #5 and #6 only, practicing the cross in front as illustrated on the left.

5. Now, have each handler do the entire sequence of #1 through #8. Allow your students to use whichever crossing method they prefer. Remind them to use a strong *Come!* after jump #7 to turn the dog off to #8. Make sure handlers give their dogs liberal praise and treats at the end of the sequence. Repeat this sequence several times.

Set 2

Your set consists of two exercises that use the same equipment. No equipment movement is required.

You'll be working with contact obstacles in your set. Remember that your students should reward their dogs only in the contact zone of the descent ramps. The dog is not permitted to leave the contact zone without a quiet release from his handler. If the dog bails off early he should be picked up and placed back on the contact zone.

In this seventh week of the intermediate program, you should encourage your students to complete the contact obstacles without giving the dog a treat on the down-side contact every time. Instead, they will treat the dog in the down-side contacts on *every other* repetition. Whether or not food is being used for a particular repetition, remind your students that they should still ask the dog for an attentive wait in the contact zones.

Don't forget that you should be making note of those dogs that should be moving on to a more advanced class and those that should repeat this intermediate program.

WEEK 7

Working the Outside

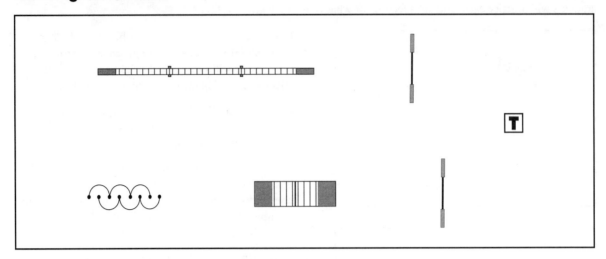

In this exercise, you will continue to work on solid performance on contact obstacles, the weave poles, and a *Down!* on the table. At the same time, you will introduce a new concept to your students. In this sequence you will require your students to work both the inside and the outside of a loop of obstacles.

In the interest of making the best use of the time you have with each group, for each repetition put the dog in a *Down!* on the table only briefly, and then release and finish the set.

1. Work the inside of the loop. With the dog on his left, each handler performs the following sequence: dogwalk–jump–table–jump–A-frame–weave poles.

    This is a relatively straightforward sequence. With the dog working on the heel-side, both dog and handler should be comfortable with the working relationship.

2. Again work the inside of the loop. This time with the dog on his right, each handler performs the following sequence: weave poles–A-frame–jump–table–jump–dogwalk.

    With the dog on the off-side, the weave poles may pose a problem for some handlers and their dogs.

3. Now work the outside of the loop. With the dog on his right, each handler performs the following sequence: dogwalk–jump–table–jump–A-frame–weave poles.

    The difficulty in performing this sequence is that the handler will be on the dog's left when a right turn is required after the jump following the dogwalk. Advise your students simply to cross and push towards the table. The dog will follow. Again, the dog will have to perform the weave poles on the off-side.

4. Again work the outside of the loop. This time with the dog on his left, each handler performs the following sequence: weave poles–A-frame–jump–table–jump–dogwalk.

    The difficulty in this sequence is that the handler will be on the dog's right when a left turn is required after the jump following the A-frame. Advise your students simply to cross and push towards the table. The dog will follow.

To Boldly Go

In this exercise, you will use the same obstacles in the same position as for the "Working the Outside" exercise.

The purpose of this exercise is to teach your students to lead out while their dogs are in a stay on the table. The advantage of leading out away from the table is that it allows the handler to get an advantageous position to begin the sequence.

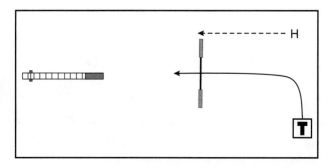

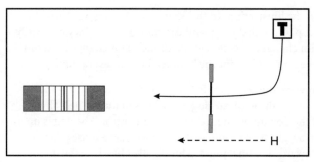

1. Have the handler *Down!* his dog on the table and command him to *Stay!*.

2. The handler then leads out to the jump on the dogwalk side of the loop as shown in the illustration on the left. This will give the handler position to handle the rest of the sequence with the dog on the heel-side.

3. The handler calls his dog to him and then performs the jump and dogwalk.

4. Repeat steps 1–3 with each of your students and then change the sequence and perform steps 5–7.

5. Have the handler *Down!* his dog on the table and command him to *Stay!*.

6. The handler then leads out to the jump on the A-frame side of the loop as shown in the illustration on the left. This will give the handler position to handle the rest of the sequence with the dog on the off-side.

7. The handler calls his dog to him and then performs: jump–A-frame–weave poles.

If the dog breaks his stay, the handler should return to the dog and make a correction by placing the dog back down on the table and repeating his *Stay!* command.

Set 3

Your set consists of two exercises that use the same equipment. However, some minor equipment movement will be required between exercises.

You'll be working with contact obstacles in your set. Remember that your students should reward their dogs only in the contact zone of the descent ramps. The dog is not permitted to leave the contact zone without a quiet release from his handler. If the dog bails off early he should be picked up and placed back on the contact zone.

At this stage in the intermediate program, you should encourage your students to complete the contact obstacles without giving the dog a treat on the down-side contact every time. Instead, they will treat the dog in the down-side contacts on *every other* repetition. Whether or not food is being used for a particular repetition, remind your students that they should still ask the dog for a good long, attentive wait in the contact zones.

Don't forget that you should be making note of those dogs that should be moving on to a more advanced class and those that should repeat this intermediate program.

The Wave

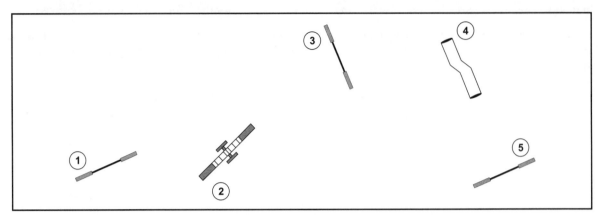

The purpose of this exercise is to work on the dog's attention to the handler. The sequence features two changes of direction. The handler will manage those changes of direction by getting his dog's attention.

1. Each handler runs the sequence, #1–#5, as shown in the illustration. In this sequence, the dog will turn left after jump #1 to the see-saw. Have handlers lead out past the first jump and call the dog over. They can easily turn and direct the dog to the see-saw. The dog again changes direction at the tunnel. This change is accomplished as the dog enters the tunnel, which should be no problem for the handler. Repeat several times.

2. Reverse the direction of the see-saw so that you can work the sequence in the opposite direction, #5–#1. In this new direction, the handler has an opportunity to get ahead of the dog while he is in the tunnel. The handler can then call the dog over jump #3 and set the dog up on the see-saw under control. The dog is on the handler's right at the down-side of the see-saw with a right turn required after the see-saw. Advise your students simply to push across the dog's path and towards the final jump. This is called **heading** the dog. Repeat this sequence several times.

Turn Backs

In this exercise, you'll continue with what has become a common theme: getting control of the dog and calling him out of a sequence. In this case, your students will be especially challenged because the tunnel will be a powerful attraction to many dogs. Allow handlers to work the dog on the heel-side.

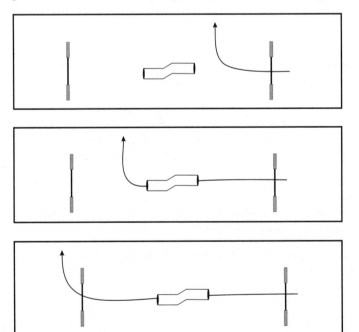

Each dog and handler will do *all* of the following steps *before* the next dog and handler in line work the exercise:

1. The handler puts the dog over the first jump in the sequence and then calls the dog out. The handler should praise the dog and give him a treat.

2. The handler puts the dog over the jump and through the tunnel, and then calls the dog out of the sequence. The handler should praise the dog and give him a food treat.

3. The handler performs the entire sequence and then calls the dog out to the side. The handler should praise the dog and give him a food treat.

If time permits, repeat the exercise with the dog working on the handler's right.

Week 7: Student Notes

It should be clear by now how important food motivators are for teaching agility obstacles and concepts to your dog. However, when teaching the dog to spur on for greater speed, there are two essential tools: tennis shoes and toys.

Speed should become part of the dog's curriculum *earlier* rather than later so that the dog doesn't become fixed at the handler's pace. All dogs are faster than their humans. A sluggish agility performance is something that has to be learned.

As soon as your dog understands the basic job—jump, tunnel, tire— it's time to strap on the tennies and see just how fast *you* can go. If your dog's performance suffers, you have to slow it down and make a programmed approach at building speed.

Ideally, your dog will be toy motivated: a ball or Frisbee™ is best for impulsion. Get your dog anticipating the performance out away from you. Then reward with the toy, pushing the dog out even more.

Artist: Nancy Krouse-Culley

Timing of the delivery is important. You don't want the dog looking or turning back to you. So, as the dog is in the air over that final jump…the toy motivator should come bouncing into view, compelling the dog on that outward path.

Older, slower, and less fit handlers can make better use of the toy motivator than running hard with the dog. Additionally, the less athletic handler can make use of smart path exercises in which the handler's path is significantly shorter than the dog's path.

Tunnel Basics

If you haven't yet added a tunnel to your set of backyard obstacles, it's time to do it now! If you haven't been able to find a suitable children's play tunnel, you're going to have to improvise. Find yourself a paper, plastic, or metal barrel and cut the bottom out of it. Make sure that the barrel is clean and safe, with no sharp edges protuding. The barrel should also be washed thoroughly—barrels are often used to store detergents and other agents which might be irritating to the dogs. Car washes are often good sources of barrels and sometimes you'll see newspaper ads for used "juice barrels". You can also check the Yellow Pages for companies that sell used barrels.

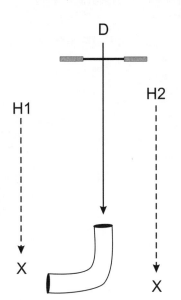

In this drill, you are going to work on calling your dog over a jump and directing the dog into a tunnel. The ultimate objective is for you to be able to stand behind the tunnel and call the dog to you over the jump, and then direct the dog through the tunnel.

- Leave the dog in a *Stay!* behind the jump. Lead out to position H1 as shown in the illustration and then call the dog over the jump. Turn around and run with the dog on your left to the tunnel. Praise and treat the dog after the tunnel.

- Leave the dog in a *Stay!* behind the jump. Lead out to position H2 as shown in the illustration and then call the dog over the jump. Turn around and run with the dog on your right to the tunnel. Praise and treat the dog after the tunnel.

- Repeat this exercise alternating which side of the sequence you work on. If the dog is doing well, gradually increase your lead-out along the dashed lines shown in the illustration. Ultimately you want to work up to being able to lead out to each position marked "X"; however, this should be done very gradually over the course of the week.

Wind Sprints

While it is important to teach our dogs to work away from us, most of the time in agility you are going to be *running with* your dog. Since most dogs will run only as fast as their handlers, this poses a problem for you. You're going to have to work a little harder to get the necessary speed out of your dog.

The following game will help you get used to running with your dog and will also help you push the dog for more speed. All you need for the initial stages of the game are a bunch of your dog's favorite treats and a plastic container (without a cover) that will be readily visible to the dog in the grass. A 1 lb. deli container like the ones that they put potato salad in at the grocery store works very well. The best time to play this game is before your dog eats his regular meal, since he'll be hungry and extra motivated for the food.

- Turn the container upside down and place a food treat underneath it. Allow your dog to see you doing this. You may also want to talk to your dog while you're placing the treat to get him even more excited—"Look what I've got here for you! Do you want to get it!"

- Take the dog and walk about 30' away from the container in a straight line. Hold the dog by the collar, point to the treat again (hopefully, the dog is lunging towards the container by now!), say "Ready! Set! Go!" and release the dog. As you let the dog go, you take off with him towards the container.

- The first one to the container wins. If the dog gets there first, he gets to knock the container over and get the treat (help the dog tip the container if he's unsure). If you win, pick up the container and show the dog what he missed out on—hold him by the collar and let him sniff the treat and get excited, but don't let him have it. You'll take the dog back and try it again.

- After a couple tries from 30', start the race 50' back from the container.

NOTE: The purpose of this game is to motivate the dog and get both of you running hard. However, there are some handlers who are much faster than their dogs even when the dogs are running at top speed. This is particularly true in the case of very small dogs who have to take a lot more strides to keep up with their humans. If your dog is trying his best and you're getting better speed out of him in this racing exercise, but you're still consistently beating him to the container, then let him win a race every now and then. You don't want to teach the dog that he can never win as this will discourage him from putting his best effort into the race.

If this game is going well over the course of the week, add a jump halfway between the starting line and the container. The rules remain the same.

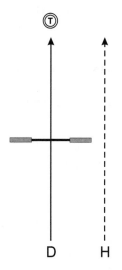

Week 8: Instructor Notes

There are two reasons that a dog will not respond to a command: 1) the dog is uncertain or fearful; or 2) the dog is distracted or feels he has a choice.

Take note that nowhere in this list is "The dog is willful and chooses to ignore his handler." But this is the reason that many people will give their dogs a harsh correction: "He knows better than that!" They say, "He knows what he's supposed to do!"

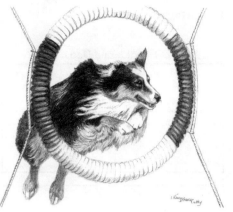

It takes some skill to recognize what the dog is experiencing. The equally skillful trainer will understand what to do about it. There's never really an excuse for a harsh correction. And in some cases, a correction isn't necessary at all. Let's break it down:

Artist: Nancy Krouse-Culley

You want to HELP a dog that is confused or afraid:

- Redesign the training problem so the dog cannot make a mistake.

- Use lots of praise when the dog succeeds.

- Break the exercise down into small steps.

- Repeat the exercise until you are certain the dog understands the desired behavior.

You want to CORRECT a dog that is distracted or feels he has a choice:

- With the dog on-lead, set up the distracting circumstance and correct the dog with a quick pop of the leash. Praise and reward the dog for turning away from the distraction and focusing his attention on the handler.

- Proof the exercise.

- With the dog on-lead, set up a circumstance where the dog is likely to make the mistake. When necessary, correct the dog with a quick pop of the leash. Praise and reward the dog for focusing on the handler.

- Repeat the exercise in unique environments.

	Set 1	Set 2	Set 3
Week 8	**Dynamic Cross** **Blind to Long Jump** *Obstacles Required:* Dogwalk, long jump see-saw, weave poles, three winged jumps, collapsed tunnel *Note:* Minor equipment movement is required between exercises.	**Perch in the Speed Circle** **Sheep Shank** 🐾 *Obstacles Required:* three winged jumps, spread hurdle, table *Note:* Minor equipment movement is required between exercises.	**Ready Freddy!** **Freddy Inside Out** 🐾 *Obstacles Required:* A-frame, pipe tunnel, tire, two winged jumps *Note:* Minor equipment movement is required between exercises.

Organizational Notes

This is your last week of class. Be sure to tell your students how wonderful it was to have them in your class. Let them know how and when they will be notified regarding who will move up to the advanced program and who should repeat the intermediate program.

Start the training session by doing the control exercise on page 103 with *all* students. Then break into groups for the training sets, if you're going to work multiple sets simultaneously.

Note that all of the sets will require minor equipment movement between exercises.

Week 8: Progress Worksheet

Instructors: **Date:**

Handler and Dog	Present	Notes

GENERAL NOTES:

Week 8: Facility Layout

One square = 10'

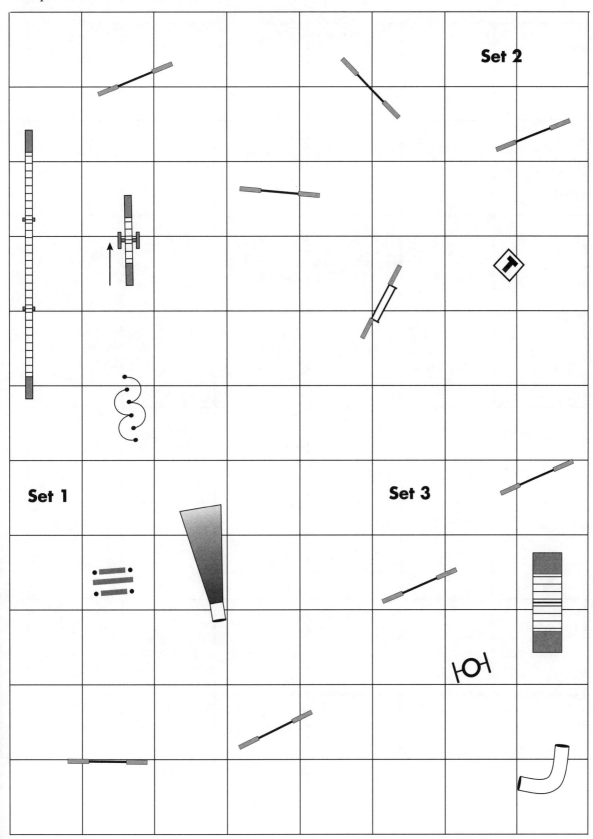

WEEK 8

Week 8: Facility Layout Worksheet

Design your Facility Layout using a 1" = 10' scale (standard agility template)

Week 8: Exercises

Start the class by doing the control exercise with everyone. Then break into smaller groups if you're going to work the training sets simultaneously.

Control Exercise

Start this class with an obedience warm-up exercise. Dogs will work on leash. This is a simple citizenship test. Handlers should take care that their dogs don't lunge at other dogs or their handlers.

- Heel the dogs on-leash into the field away from the equipment.

- Form two lines of the same number of dogs and handlers. Both lines will face the same direction.

- Have both lines of dogs and handlers heel forward. The lines will turn and heel into each other. Handlers with their dogs will weave in and out of the line of dogs approaching them.

End of exercise.

Set 1

Your set consists of two exercises that use largely the same equipment. Some equipment movement is required between exercises, but that movement is relatively minor.

Balance your time with each group so that your students get approximately the same amount of work on each of the exercises.

You'll be working with contact obstacles in your set. Remember that your students should reward their dogs only in the contact zone of the descent ramps. The dog is not permitted to leave the contact zone without a quiet release from his handler. If the dog bails off early he should be picked up and placed back on the contact zone.

As you did last week, you should encourage your students to complete the contact obstacles without giving the dog a treat on the down-side contact every time.

Dynamic Cross

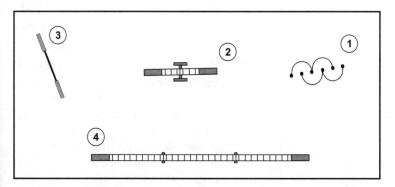

A **dynamic cross** is executed while the dog is committed to an obstacle with the handler in plain sight. In this exercise:

- Do *not* permit the handler to lead out from the dog.

- The handler will start the sequence at the weave poles with the dog on his left.

- After the dog has committed to the jump at #3, the handler will cross behind the dog so that the dog will be on the off-side for the dogwalk.

If the dog is unused to the idea of the handler changing sides, it may elect to pull off the jump before committing. So it's up to the handler to *sell* the dog on going ahead to the jump. This is where all of your work sending the dog out to do a jump will pay off.

The dogs should be waiting in the down-side yellow of both contact obstacles for the handler's quiet release. Tell your students *not* to give the dog a treat in the contact, but be prepared to give the dog praise and a treat each time the dog completes the sequence, in either direction. This will be a good test of all of your careful work with the dog on these contact obstacles.

Blind to Long Jump

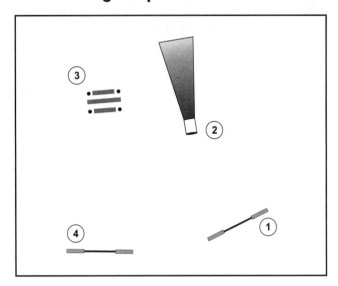

The long jump should be regularly featured in your agility training program. Many instructors choose not to use the long jump because it's more difficult and time consuming to adjust than a standard bar jump, but it's worth the effort in the long run.

This sequence features a blind turn to the long jump—the dog will be exiting the collapsed tunnel at #2 and then needs to turn left to the long jump at #3.

Do not allow your students to lead out.

Run the exercise several times.

Set 2

Your set consists of two exercises that use largely the same equipment. Some equipment movement is required between exercises, but that movement is relatively minor. You'll be using the spread hurdle. Please refer to page 110 in the Appendix for a discussion of the height and depth at which the bars need to be set.

Balance your time with each group so that your students get approximately the same amount of work on each exercise.

The "Sheep-Shank" exercise is somewhat advanced. If your students are struggling with the exercise, you might want to simplify it so that you end on a positive note.

Perch in the Speed Circle

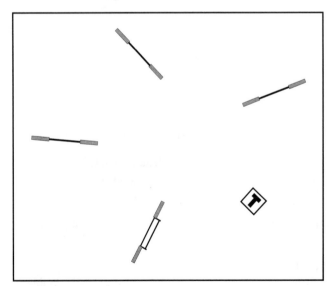

This spread hurdle in this speed circle is set so that the handler is allowed the inside path and can move through execution of the spread with a prompt and purposeful stride.

Often, when a dog is having difficulty with the spread, the handler's cues (posture and stride) may be a part of the problem. Freddy's handler, for instance, worries so much about the spread that when he encounters it in competition, he will slow down, shorten his stride, and rotate his frame perpendicular to the flow. Freddy will then vindicate his handler's worrying and oblige him by crashing the bars on the spread.

In each repetition, the dog will start and stop on the table. Ask for a good *Down!* on the table. The instructor should count for the dog.

1. With the dog on his right, each handler runs the circle in a counterclockwise direction. Repeat this sequence several times.

2. Next turn the spread hurdle around and reverse the direction of the flow. With the dog on his left, each handler runs the circle in a clockwise direction. The handler should make sure the dog has a clean approach to the spread hurdle. Repeat this sequence several times.

Sheep Shank 🐾

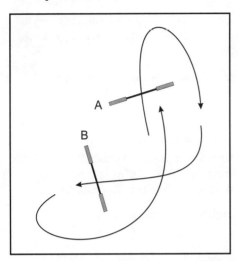

This exercise introduces your intermediate students to a dramatic change of direction. Your students should be prepared to use plenty of treats and praise. It's important for the dog to love this exercise and to learn that changing direction can be fun.

The exercise will also teach your students an important lesson in body position. Taking the tight, inside position and turning is probably not the best handling strategy for 180˚and 270˚turns.

It is important in this exercise that the handler never turns his back on the dog.

Try to visualize these steps:

1. Starting with the dog on his left, the handler sends his dog over jump A.

2. The handler steps right, laterally, and calls the dog around the right wing of jump A.

3. As the dog is returning to him, the handler rotates his body counterclockwise to face jump B. The dog is now on the handler's right.

4. The handler sends his dog over jump B.

5. The handler steps left, laterally, and calls the dog around the left wing of jump B.

6. As the dog is returning to him, the handler rotates his body clockwise to face jump A. The dog is back on the handler's left again.

7. The handler sends his dog over jump A again.

It would be very useful for you to demonstrate the movements required in this exercise.

Set 3

Your set consists of two exercises that use largely the same equipment. Some equipment movement is required between exercises, but that movement is relatively minor.

Balance your time with each group so that your students get approximately the same amount of work on each of the exercises.

The Freddy Inside Out exercise is somewhat advanced. If your intermediate students are struggling with the exercise, you might want to simplify it so that you end on a positive note. The exercise can be redesigned into a simple looping sequence.

Ready Freddy!

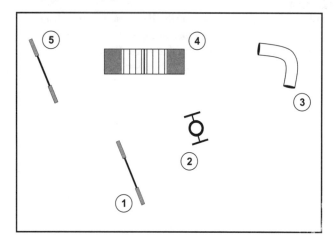

This exercise is bi-directional. You are going to have your students run it several times in both directions.

The dogs should be waiting in the down-side yellow of the A-frame for the handler's quiet release. Tell your students *not* to give the dog a treat in the contact, but be prepared to give the dog praise and a treat each time the dog completes the sequence, in either direction. This will be a good test of all of your careful work with the dog on these contact obstacles.

Do *not* allow your students to lead out.

1. With the dog starting on his left side, each handler performs the sequence #1–#5. The handler should be prepared to change sides in front of the tunnel so that the dog is on the handler's right side when it comes out of the tunnel. Point out to anyone who runs around the tunnel that taking that long path slows the dog down. Both the handler and the dog should get used to the possibility that the handler will change sides from time to time. Repeat this sequence several times.

2. Now each handler runs the sequence in the other direction, #5–#1. Repeat this sequence several times.

Freddy Inside Out

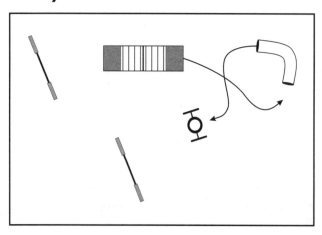

Using the same set of obstacles, challenge your students with putting the dog in the *alternate side* of the pipe tunnel.

Throughout the intermediate program, one of your major themes has been to teach the handlers to get control of the dog between obstacles. The dog should *not* automatically commit to the obstacle in front of him without a directive from his handler to do so.

In this exercise, the handler will call his dog to him after performance of the obstacle prior to the tunnel (either the A-frame or the tire, depending on which direction the exercise is being run). The handler needs to keep the dog's attention while moving towards the alternate entrance to the tunnel, and away from the more obvious and direct entrance.

The illustration shows performance of the tunnel after the A-frame. This should be quite easy for your students because you always ask them to have control of their dogs in the contact zone before releasing the dog. In this instance, tell your students to use *Come!* as the release from the contact.

When you run the set in the opposite direction, however, the dog will be moving faster and with more obvious flow. Your students should use the *Come!* command to get control of their dogs and move across to the correct entry to the tunnel.

WEEK 8

Week 8: Student Notes

The real beauty of running a dog in agility comes from that special bond that allows you and your dog to run together, flawlessly through the most complicated courses. You get there not only by virtue of sheer numbers of repetitions of basic drills; but in working on many different kinds of combinations of obstacle sequences, and working out the problematical puzzles before you actually see them in competition. (Or certainly if you are a thinking trainer, you'll work the puzzle before seeing it *twice* in competition.)

We have perhaps made the language of dog agility too complicated already. We struggle to find words to describe simple maneuvers. A *counter-rotation*, for instance, is merely turning around and heading in a new direction; a *dynamic cross* is switching from one side of your dog to the

Artist: Valerie Pietraszewska

other while both of you are running. And while the word we choose to describe it is technical and intellectual, the act or event itself is purely instinctual and physically robust. So we design exercises that are illustrative of the physical demands of the desired performance. This is the way you turn around and head in a new direction. This is the way you switch sides with your dog.

You do enough of these exercises and you *will* learn what they seek to teach you. It's often called the rule of 5,000—anything you do 5,000 times...you own.

Balancing Act

You're going to your dog to balance a food treat on his nose. This may seem like a silly parlor trick, but working with your dog to teach him any skill or trick will help improve communication between the two of you. What you are really doing is practicing how to train your dog.

This trick will be suitable for impressing friends and guests with your dog's control and dexterity. Of course, there's nothing your friends and guests would rather do than explore your dog's complete repertoire of tricks.

There are some prerequisite skills for teaching this cute little trick: 1) Your dog needs to know how to *Sit!* on command; 2) Your dog needs to know *Stay!*; and 3) Your dog needs to know a *Catch It!* command.

Catch It! is pretty easy to teach. Use small bits of food. Toss a treat to your dog saying *Catch It!* At first, you toss the tidbits directly at his face, nice and easy. Then as your dog gets good at snatching the treats out of the air, you can make the toss slightly off to the side, saying *Catch It!*. Then you can start flipping the treat up so that it arcs up in the air and drops down to the dog.

Once you have all these skills down, you're ready to start putting them together. A doggie biscuit works well for this trick because it's flat and will easily rest on your dog's nose (so long as he doesn't move!).

Start by commanding your dog to *Sit!*. Then balance the bit of food on his nose and tell him to *Stay!*. The only thing new you really need to teach your dog is the flip. Reach over to your dog with both hands, who has patiently waited as you balanced this food on his nose, and use both index fingers to flip the food into the air, saying *Catch It!* as you do so.

Do this several times and your dog will begin flipping his own nose up to make the catch. You can gradually remove yourself from the equation. So the trick becomes: *Sit! — Stay!* — Balance the food — *Catch It!*.

Good luck!

Turning Back

You've been working for weeks learning to call your dog out of a sequence and reverse the flow. In this exercise, we take a logical leap to the next step; that is, turning your dog to perform another obstacle, in a completely different direction.

- In the first exercise, you will put your dog over two jumps and then call him around the second jump. Practice calling your dog around the jump in *both* directions as shown in Figures 1 and 2.

- In the next exercise, you are going to perform each jump twice as shown in Figure 3. You will first turn the dog right and then you will turn him left. You should also try working the reverse, so that you turn the dog left first and then right as shown in Figure 4.

- In this last exercise, you are going to perform each jump twice as shown in Figure 5. You will turn the dog right both times. Also try the exercise turning the dog left both times as shown in Figure 6.

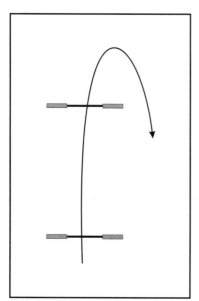

Figure 1

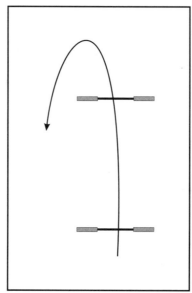

Figure 2

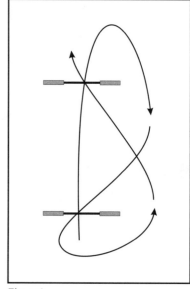

Figure 3

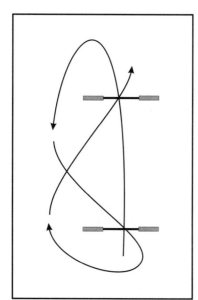

Figure 4

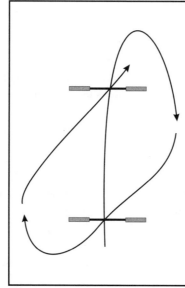

Figure 5

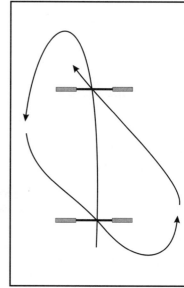

Figure 6

Appendix

Additional Guidelines for Program Design

Introducing Spread Hurdles

Remedial Work Reference

Artist: Bud Houston

Additional Guidelines for Program Design

A good training program is always evolving. You and your instructors should meet regularly to review your training procedures and exercises, and to evaluate their effectiveness. The only way to discover what works and what doesn't work is to try out your ideas and carefully observe the results. When you design a new exercise does it accomplish the goal(s) you intended? Do your instructors understand the goal(s) of the exercise and are they comfortable running the set? How does the exercise work for the students? Is it over their heads? Is it too easy?

Throughout this workbook, we have suggested a number of guidelines for designing and structuring your intermediate agility program. Here are a few other guidelines to keep in mind as you refine your program:

• Don't try to design a set of exercises that's going to fix everyone's problems. It can't be done in an hour.

• Keep a training log of what the class has worked on lately. This will alert you as to obstacles and common obstacle configurations that you haven't worked on lately. For example, it's very easy to forget to set out the long jump. Then you and your students go to a trial where the judge seems determined to make up for all those other trials where he didn't use the long jump.

• After class while it is still fresh, confer with the other instructors and see if there is any pattern to the problems you are observing with the class. For example, if many dogs in the class are slow on the see-saw or knocking bars on the spread hurdle or can only make correct entry into the weaves if they are stopped or slowed down before the obstacle, you know that you have been neglecting this in your program. It is not a bad idea to keep notes on the individual students either. This can act as a rough metric so that you can determine whether or not your class is making progress in those long months between trial seasons.

• Keep copies of courses you have seen at trials. If you are having trouble thinking up a training pattern, these can be a good source of inspiration. Also, when designing exercise sets, it's easy to unconsciously lock yourself into using certain configurations; or not using certain configurations because you think of them as "unfair". Unfair or not, you and/or your students are going to see them at trial somewhere, so you may as well "Train, Don't Complain" as Jack Godsil used to say.

• Ask your students for feedback about what they liked and didn't like during the eight weeks. It's a good idea to develop an evaluation form that you give students on the last day of class.

Introducing Spread Hurdles

For the purposes of this training program, a spread hurdle should consist of two individual bar jumps placed closely together with the front bar set somewhat lower than the back bar. The reason for using two individual jumps rather than a fixed oxer or spread hurdle is so that you have complete control over the distance between the front and back bars.

In the intermediate program, it is *not* important to increase the height and width of the spread hurdle so that it is as high and deep as the dog must ultimately jump in competition. Rather, it is only necessary to introduce the dog to the concept that a jump will occasionally have a dimension of depth.

Throughout this program, you should use no more than three jump settings: the back bar will be set at either 6", 12", or 18". Use the following table to determine the height of the front bar and the distance between the front and back bars.

Height of Back Bar	Height of Front Bar	Distance Between Bars
6"	3"	3"
12"	6"	6"
18"	12"	12"

If you do not have bar jumps that adjust in 1" increments, when the lower setting of 3" is required, use aluminum soda cans to prop up the front bar. Lay the cans perpendicular to the bar and press the bar down so that the cans form a depression cup to hold the bar. This will give you approximately 3" in elevation and allows the bar to be easily displaceable in case the dog lands on it or runs into it.

Remedial Work Reference

It is very common for dogs to have problems with particular obstacles during an intermediate training program—after all, they are still in the process of learning. However, it is in the intermediate program that you want to resolve these problems and get the dog performing all of the obstacles happily and correctly.

Use this reference as a source of ideas when you are at your wit's end. There is no one right answer for all dogs, even though your students will look to you for those answers. You have to learn to observe and to be creative when coming up with possible solutions for any problem.

Bill Sterling, an agility instructor for B.R.A.G. in the Columbus, Ohio area, tells a story of one of his students whose dog's see-saw performance was painfully slow. The dog would inch forward on the see-saw so carefully that it used up 15 or 20 seconds getting over the obstacle. Then one day while Bill was watching the dog doing its usual see-saw performance, the handler bent down to pick up something that had dropped on the ground. As the handler bent down, Bill noticed that the dog immediately dropped its head and moved forward, and the plank dropped. Bill advised this handler to try, *just try*, bending over at the waist as her dog got to the balance point on the see-saw. The handler pooh-poohed the idea, but she tried it none-the-less just to show Bill that he was wrong. But magically, the dog repeated the head-dropping action and forward motion behavior, and it got over the see-saw in short seconds. The handler has used the bend-at-the-waist maneuver ever since to get over the see-saw, and it has worked.

The moral of this story is that the instructor must learn to be a keen observer and to sometimes come up with some creative solutions for mysterious problems.

CAUTION: When evaluating any obstacle problem—particularly problems that involve a reluctance to jump or scale—it is important to rule out any physical problem before you assume that it is a training problem. If you are even slightly suspicious that a dog might be trying to avoid performance of an obstacle because of a physical problem, you should ask the handler to have the dog thoroughly examined by a veterinarian before you start looking for a training solution. Obesity is a common physical problem to look for as it can cause many obstacle performance problems. For example, Monica Percival had a dog come for a private lesson because according to the handler, the dog would run one class brilliantly and then get "lazy and careless" in the next class. The dog would knock bars, run around jumps, and even sometimes go hide in the tunnel. Upon a visual and then hands-on examination of the dog, Monica advised the handler that the dog was at least 20 lbs. overweight and also out of shape. There were no magical training solutions to this problem, the dog needed to go on a diet and a regular routine of exercise.

NOTE: The three-dimensional renderings of the obstacles pictured in this section were created by Pascal Peng.

Jumps and Hurdles

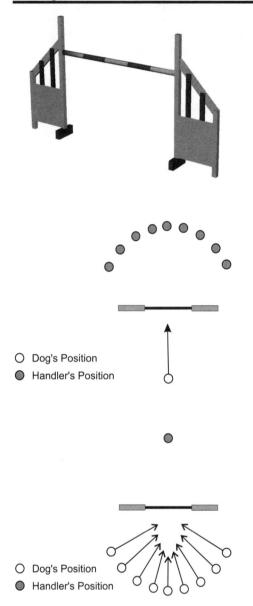

Dog's Position ○
Handler's Position ●

Dog's Position ○
Handler's Position ●

A refusal on a jump is running past the jump without jumping over, jumping between the bars when two bars are used, running under the bars, jumping the wing of a winged jump, or coming to a stop in front of the jump.

- Try reducing the height of the jump. If the dog jumps the reduced height happily, put the dog on a program in which the jump height is raised only an inch or two each week.

- Use a spotter to hold the dog in front of the jump. The handler goes to the opposite side of the jump and coaxes the dog over with a food treat or toy motivator. Do this until the dog is happily jumping over the hurdle to get to his handler.

- Make sure the handler is using a clear hand signal that is within the dog's field of vision.

- A basic "what is the job" exercise would be helpful. Have the handler work on calling the dog over a jump in an "around the clock manner". The dog is left with a spotter (or on a *Stay!* if reliable) at the six o' clock position. On each repetition, the handler moves to a different position as shown in the first illustration on the left. The handler should call the dog over the jump using a voice command and a good hand signal, and he should give immediate praise and reward as the dog lands. Try the call-over exercise with the handler remaining stationary at the twelve o'clock position and the dog being placed at a different position on each repetition as shown in the second illustration on the left. The handler should also work on sending the dog to a jump. This can be done in an around-the-clock manner with the handler and dog starting together at the same position, working their way around the clock. Consistent application of reward is vitally important so that the dog will figure out the performance that gets him the reward and the performance for which reward is denied.

Knocked bars are also a frequent performance problem with jumps.

- Reduce the dog's jump height. Put the handler on a program to increase the jump height gradually, only one or two inches every week or two.

- Some dogs are "lazy" jumpers and don't particularly care if their feet hit and knock bars. Suspend a rubber band, nylon string, or fishing line so that it is taut between the jump uprights, about an inch above the jump bar. If the dog drops his back feet, he will graze the material above the bar. Most dogs don't like the feeling of something touching their toes and will lift their legs and put more effort into clearing the bar. You can also use a heavier pole on the jump (for example, you can fill a PVC pole with sand and cap the ends). If the pole gives the dog an unpleasant rap on the toes, the dog will be less lazy about getting up and over.

- Conditioning might be a problem. You could prescribe a regimen of roadwork for the handler and dog.

- Watch to see if the handler is slowing down, or even stopping as the dog commits towards the jump. This can cause the dog to slow down or shorten its stride, causing a knocked bar. The handler should be alongside the dog when the dog jumps, if at all possible.

APPENDIX

- Does the dog tend to knock bars when the handler crosses behind him? Dogs that aren't completely comfortable with their handlers crossing behind them will tend to turn in mid-air to locate their handler, dropping their back feet in the process. Work on more crossing exercises and have the handler try to cross in front of the dog rather than behind the dog whenever possible.

- Jump the dog at a slightly greater height in practice than in competition. For example, if the dog is used to jumping 26" in practice, the dog will be unlikely to knock bars when jumping 24" in competition.

- Pay attention to the timing of the handler's commands. Some dogs inadvertently learn to actually jump at the moment the handler gives the *Jump!* command rather than evaluating a proper take-off for themselves. Because the dog takes off too early or too late based on the timing of the command, he frequently knocks bars. Some basic send-away to a jump and "learn the job" exercises would be a good idea.

- We tend to assume that dogs are "natural" jumpers. In many cases, this is not true and the dog has trouble determining where to take off to clear the jumps cleanly. This dog needs to be *trained* to jump well. Working with ground poles and a jumping chute (a straight line of six to eight jumps) can be very helpful for teaching the dog to judge his proper take-off points. There are a number of books available on working with jumping chutes and changing a dog's jumping style; for example, *Jumping from A to Z* by M. Christine Zink and Julie Daniels and *The Clothier Natural Jumping Method* by Suzanne Clothier.

- Place a line of aluminum cans below the jump where the bar would fall if the dog displaces it. The cans should set up a clatter that will alarm the dog, presumably making the dog less likely to want the bar to fall again.

- For spread hurdles, the handler might adopt a command that communicates to the dog that the jump has a dimension of depth. Often dogs cannot fathom that a jump is depth as well as height, so a handler might say *Big Jump!* to remind the dog to push a little harder to get up and over.

Tire Jump

A refusal on the tire is running past without jumping through the tire aperture, jumping between the tire and the frame, or coming to a stop in front of the tire.

- Use a spotter to hold the dog in front of the tire. Pass the dog's lead through the tire. The handler should go to the opposite side and coax the dog through the tire with a food treat or toy motivator. Do this until the dog is happily diving through the tire to his handler. The spotter should only release the dog if he's going to go through the aperture. If the dog attempts to go between the tire and the frame, the spotter should use the leash to prevent him from doing this.

- Try reducing the height of the tire. Put the dog on a program in which the tire height is raised gradually and incrementally.

- The dog may not understand the basic job required. An around-the-clock exercise like that illustrated on page 112 would be useful. The handler should work on both sending and calling the dog from different approaches around the clock. Consistent application of reward is important so that the dog will figure out the performance that gets it the reward and the performance for which reward is denied.

- For a dog that consistently attempts to jump between the tire and the frame, use some plastic wrap to make that space impassable to the dog. The dog will get an unexpected correction the first time he tries to jump through the plastic wrap.

- Use what is called a lollipop tire. This is a tire that is supported by means of a single pole. There is no frame to confuse the dog. When the dog understands the job of "finding the hole", try the tire in the frame again.

Long Jump

A refusal on the long jump is running past without jumping over, jumping from side to side or from front to one of the sides, or coming to a stop in front of the jump.

Other possible performance problems are a dog that walks over the planks, knocks a plank over, or just tics a plank with a toenail. In competition, these performances are scored identically to a knocked bar on a bar jump.

- Place a bar jump in between each of the long jump planks. The bars on the jumps should be set only slightly higher than the long jump planks. This will make the dog jump higher to clear the span of the long jump.

- Shorten the long jump span so that it isn't so intimidating to the dog. Over a period of weeks, gradually increase the span of the jump to the dog's competition length.

- The handler needs to use body motion to help push the dog at top speed over the long jump. Watch for the handler slowing down or hanging back as the dog goes on to do the long jump. Advise the handler to run as much as possible with the dog and, if possible, get in front of the dog for performance of the long jump.

- Use a spotter to hold the dog in front of the long jump. The handler goes to the opposite side and coaxes the dog over with a food treat or toy motivator. Make sure the dog has plenty of room to get up speed for the obstacle. Do this until the dog is happily diving over the long jump to his handler.

- Try using a plastic wrap along the sides of the long jump in practice. The four corner poles need to be set very securely in the ground. The plastic wrap will give the dog an automatic correction if the dog attempts to enter or exit through the sides.

Table

A refusal on the table is running past the table without attempting to get on, running underneath the table, or running past the table and mounting from behind. If the dog is refusing the table, try any of the following:

- With the dog on-lead, put him on the table several times, giving him lots of praise and treats.

- Have a spotter hold the dog and put the handler on the opposite side of the table. Get the handler to sit on the table and call the dog to him. Praise and treat the dog.

- Do a lot of send-to-table exercises with the extremely reluctant dog. Use targeting (preferably food) to reward the dog for getting on the table.

- If a dog comes to a complete stop in front of the table, it's possible that the table is too high. Try lowering the table for a while until the dog is more comfortable jumping at the lower height. Then you can work on raising the table height.

Skipping on and off the table is faulted in competition.

- Work on an *Easy!* command on the flat, away from any obstacles. The handler can use this command if the dog is building up too much speed on the approach to the table.

- Have the handler try to hang back and let the dog go ahead of him on the approach to the table. The dog's speed will usually start to taper off as the handler slows down.

- Try putting the table up against a wall or a tall fence so that the dog has nowhere to go beyond the table. A dog will learn quickly to measure his stride getting to the table. Make sure to keep this kind of remedy absolutely safe.

- Teach the dog to make a "U-turn" back towards the handler as the dog is jumping onto the table. This helps slow the dog's momentum onto the table and is also useful for helping to keep the dog from skidding off a slippery table. With the dog on the ground next to the table, hold a treat in both of your hands, using the thumb and index finger of *each* hand. Hold the treat in front of the dog's nose and then command *Table!*. Keeping the treat directly in front of the dog's nose as he jumps onto the table, fully extend your arms towards the back of the table and then bring your hands back towards you in a "U" shape. The dog should be following the treat the whole way. Eventually, jumping onto the table, turning around, and assuming a down position all become one motion for the dog.

- Do a lot of random drops on the flat, away from any obstacles. A handler could use a *Lie Down!* command as the dog is committing to the table. The dog should make an extra effort to come to a stop in order to lie down on the table. The handler's timing of the command will be important if the dog is to stop in time.

- Sometimes if a dog is skipping on and off the table, the table may be set at a lower height than his regulation height. Don't be too alarmed at a dog that doesn't recognize a very short platform as a table.

- Test your down-stays on the table. While the dog is down on the table, hold a treat about 4" above his nose. Most dogs will raise their elbows off the table in an attempt to get the treat. Quietly, tell the dog *Wrong* and gently place him back in the down position. Repeat this until the dog will keep his elbows down until you count to three. Immediately, release the dog and give him the reward. As the dog improves at the game, ask him to hold the down-stay for longer and longer before you release him and give him the treat.

- Set up several jumps before the table. Have the handler perform the jumps and then purposely run by the table after he commands the dog to go to the table. If the dog skips on and off the table in order to follow the handler, the handler should pick up the dog and place him in a down position on the table. If the dog stops on the table by himself, the handler should immediately praise and reward.

Weave Poles

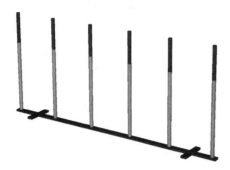

One of the hardest obstacles in dog agility to train, the weave poles present a number of possible performance problems. In the USDAA, weave pole performance faults are differentiated as a refusal, improper entry, or a missed pole. In the AKC, all of these performance problems are called refusals.

Some ideas for fixing weave pole performance include:

- Put the dog on leash. Have the handler work the dog down the line of poles. Use a food or toy if necessary to help focus the dog as he is led through the poles.

- Use channel wires to gate the proper entry and the complete performance. You could use other materials to channel the poles (a series of x-pens, chicken wire, etc). Whatever you do should be of safe construction.

- Use staggered poles to build the basic performance. Staggered poles require a channel between the poles. Odd numbered poles are set slightly to the left and even numbered poles set slightly to the right. Use targeting, and a leash if necessary, to control the dog's progress through the poles. Gradually move the poles closer and closer together to narrow the channel.

- Use leaning poles to build the basic performance. Leaning poles require the poles to be fixed in a line at the botton, but lean outward. Odd poles lean left and even poles lean right. Begin with the poles leaning outward in an exaggerated manner. Graduate the poles towards an upright position over time. The last 15° to an upright position should be very gradual so that the dog adopts a weaving motion through the poles.

- Some missed pole problems come from a dog who has been trained on only one set of poles and whose performance falls apart when he is put in a set of poles that is in any way different. As much as possible, train with different numbers of weave poles. Use an odd number once and an even number another time. If at all possible, vary the distance between weave poles from time to time. This is possible if you have a set of pound-in-the-ground poles for which you can adjust distances and the number of poles from week to week.

- The key to weave pole performance is to avoid putting stress on the dog. An emotional or physical correction could create a performance difficulty, making the dog slow and hesitant and unsure of himself. Always be attentive to the handler's attitude and tone with his dogs. Recommend using an upbeat voice, treats, and lots of praise.

- Make sure that in his attempts to be upbeat and motivate the dog, that the handler's encouragement does not turn to nagging. Some handlers make far too much noise and do too much clapping while their dog is in the poles. Often the dog will actually slow down even more. To evaluate this, have the handler run the dog through the poles without saying anything at all.

Dogwalk

A number of performance faults are possible on the dogwalk, including refusals and missed contacts.

For the dogwalk, and indeed all of the contact obstacles, the best policy is to train the dog to never be allowed to miss a contact. If the handler sticks to this rule in training, missing a contact is much less likely to become a problem in competition.

Some remedies for the dogwalk include:

- Gate the entry using x-pens, stick-in-the-ground poles, or a similar construction. The gate should be constructed so that the dog learns to square up for the entry to the dogwalk.

- Use hoops or wickets to gate the entry and exit. The wickets take away the dog's opportunity to leap up and over the ascent contact zone, and keep the dog's head down at the descent contact zone. It is generally conceded that this is only a temporary fix.

- Re-train the obstacle using a back-chaining method. The key to this method is that the dog is rewarded in the descent-side contact zone and *not* after leaving the obstacle. Also, the handler expects the dog to wait for a quiet release before leaving the obstacle.

- Picking the dog up and putting him on the obstacle can cure a dog who jumps off prematurely.

- Often a dog will race over the obstacle if he is nervous, or even frightened. Use a reduced-height obstacle for re-training. Use two spotters and control the dogs movement over the plank. Be soothing and reassuring.

- Teach the dog a command like *Wait!* or *Easy!* to slow him down into the descent side contact zone. These commands should be taught on the flat away from the obstacles.

- Give a food treat to the dog using the arm opposite of the dog and the contact. Show the food down the plank so that the dog must keep his head down and walk consistently down the plank. Use the same motion to signal to the bottom of the plank when no food is being used. The dog will put his head down and walk consistently down the plank.

- Fear of the dogwalk, or any contact obstacle, might ensue if a handler consistently allows a dog to approach the obstacle at an acute angle. Too often such an approach will cause the dog to fall off before completing the obstacle and may make the dog wary of the obstacle. Caution handlers who show insufficient respect for the approach to the obstacle.

- Physically restrain the dog on the down ramp. If applying pressure on the dog, the pressure should be on the dog's chest, pushing back up the ramp, and not to either side. This is to avoid making the dog frightened of the dogwalk.

A-Frame

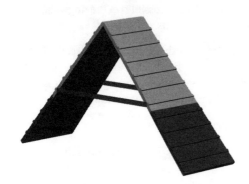

A number of performance faults are possible on the A-frame, including refusals and missed contacts.

Some remedies for the A-frame include:

- Gate the entry using x-pens or a similar construction. The gate should be constructed so that the dog learns to square up for the entry to the dogwalk.

- Reduce the height of the A-frame so that it is not so steep for the dog. Gradually raise the A-frame as the dog builds confidence and increases his speed over the obstacle.

- For a dog refusing the A-frame, get a spotter for the dog. Send the handler around to climb up on the opposite side so that his hands and face are visible to the dog. Then call the dog up and over. Many dogs will climb up after seeing their handler.

- In some cases, a dog will race his handler if the handler is rushing or surging forward. Instruct the handler to hang back a little so that the dog slows down.

- The up contact can be especially troublesome for large dogs. Some trainers have had success with teaching the dog to place a paw on a spot in the contact zone before leaping up on the obstacle. The problem with this method is that it often causes the dog to stop in front of the A-frame, earning a refusal fault. You may instead want to try placing four or five jump poles at approximately 18" to 20" intervals in front of the up ramp. These ground poles will help force the dog to shorten stride on his approach to the ramp. Over many weeks, remove one pole at a time.

- As the dog descends the A-frame, instruct the handler to spin around and face the dog, eye-ball to eye-ball, and command the dog to *Wait!* or to *Lie Down!*. This technique often works with even excitable dogs.

- Many of the remedies listed for the dogwalk also work for the A-frame.

Artist: Jaci Cotton

APPENDIX

See-Saw

A number of performance faults are possible on the see-saw, including refusals, missed contacts, and the dreaded fly-off.

Some remedies for the see-saw include:

- Use a training see-saw with an apex of about 12". Gradually raise the height of the apex.

- Use a spotter to control the board (always from behind the dog) once it tips.

- Create a gate of x-pens so that the dog has no choice but to go onto the see-saw. Give the dog a food treat at the end of the contact zone.

- Re-train see-saw performance by back-chaining. Start by picking the dog up and putting him at the down contact. Use a food reward at the end of the plank to teach the dog to focus downward. Introduce tipping using a spotter to control the plank.

- For a performance speed problem, use a plank that is over-balanced in favor of the ascent side of the see-saw in practice. When the dog encounters the see-saw in competition he'll run further out of the plank past the pivot point than he is accustomed, which will speed up performance of the obstacle considerably.

- Many of the remedies listed for the dogwalk also apply for the see-saw.

Pipe Tunnel

A refusal at the pipe tunnel occurs when the dog runs past the entrance without entering, stops at the entrance, or enters the tunnel and comes back out the entrance.

- Shorten the tunnel. Have a spotter hold the dog. Pass the dog's leash through the tunnel as the handler goes on the other side and calls the dog through.

- Put the dog on a program to reinforce the basic job—"find the hole". Shorten the tunnel, send the dog to run through from different angles and distances. Gradually lengthen the tunnel and introduce a bend. Use a lot of praise and food rewards.

- Call the dog through the tunnel and send him away through the tunnel in an around-the-clock manner as illustrated on page 112.

- Demonstrate a clear hand signal, using the hand closest to the dog, and pushing towards the tunnel.

- Set up the tunnel so it is straight and fully extended. Put the dog on a 20' long line. Place a treat or toy on a paper plate at the far end of the tunnel. Have a spotter hold on to the long line. The handler should command *Tunnel!* and run to the other side. If the dog goes directly in the tunnel entrance, the spotter should let go off the long line. If the dog tries to run around the tunnel, he corrects himself on the line.

Collapsed Tunnel

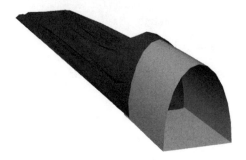

A refusal at the collapsed tunnel occurs when the dog runs past the entrance without entering, stops at the entrance, or enters the tunnel and comes back out the entrance.

- Remove the fabric chute from the tunnel. Have a spotter hold the dog. Pass the dog's leash through the tunnel as the handler goes on the other side and calls the dog through.

- Shorten the fabric chute. Have someone hold the chute open for the dog so that the dog can see daylight. After the chute is fully extended begin dropping the chute down on the dog as the dog nears the end. Begin dropping the chute earlier and earlier. Finally, let the dog push his own way through the chute without holding it open.

- Create a gate of x-pens so that the dog has no choice but to go into the tunnel. Use a food target at the tunnel exit.

Artist: Jaci Cotton

Intermediate Agility Workbook

Motivation

Artist: Jaci Cotton

One of the most difficult problems for an instructor to find an answer to is that of the dog's motivation. If a dog is working slowly or reluctantly, the source can be a variety of problems.

- It could be that the dog is not in a hurry, and can see no good reason to be in a hurry. The dog isn't particularly food motivated, praise doesn't stir him, and he doesn't care much about toys. There's not too much we can do about this dog but continue to play (if you can stand it) and hope that he one day catches fire.

- The dog that is overweight or out of shape will not be too motivated. It's easy to spot the overweight dog, though it's somewhat harder to tell the owner to quit making the dog a couch potato and to get him off his duff and get out and do some roadwork.

- A dog that is suffering pain from some physical problem may not be too keen to do agility. Hip displasia or back problems may be totally debilitating for the dog. If it's clear to you that a dog is in pain, you should advise the handler to seek counsel from his vet. Some temporary problems might also arise. Sometimes the instructor's eye is better trained to see problems with a dog than even his own handler. If a dog looks like he is hurting, then he probably is. Recommend to the handler that the dog get rested and healed.

- Some dogs run no faster than is necessary. If a handler is exceptionally slow then the dog may pace himself to match the handler's pace. Encourage the handler to move as much and as fast as possible. Put the dog on a program of going out to perform obstacles. A dog like this is often the by-product of intense obedience training. Some of that training has to be untrained.

- A handler can be too gruff with a dog, or meet the dog's failures with emotional corrections and doggie scorn. This does not help the dog get motivated to the sport. Advise this handler to lighten up and to use a lot of food or the dog's favorite toy. Get the handler using a high-pitched upbeat voice and a lot of praise.

- Use a speed circle to motivate a reluctant dog. This training plan makes that point on more than one occasion. To add a bit of spice to the speed circle, run it as a tandem or brace. Start the reluctant dog on one side of the circle and another dog on the opposite side of the circle. When you begin to jump the dogs, the race is on. A new excitement and enthusiasm for the dog might be born from this kind of exercise.

- Be sure to figure out what really turns the dog on. For some dogs, food does the trick; for others, only a toy will do. In general, food should be used to teach an obstacle, while a toy could be used to add excitement and possibly speed to the performance. Don't use toys to reward performance of a contact obstacle because the dog will be rewarded for bailing off the obstacle early. However, use the toy after a sequence of jumps and tunnels and the dog could become genuinely excited and motivated.